FABRICATING EVIDENCE II

Office of the Attorney General/Mississippi Department of Corrections Integrity Meltdown

Britton Mosley, Sr.
John "Jimmy" Fancher

Fabricating Evidence II: Office of the Attorney General/Mississippi Department of Corrections Integrity Meltdown Copyright © 2016 by Britton Mosley, Sr. & John Fancher

All rights reserved.

Published by
Mighty Monarch Publishing
P.O. Box 2036
Woodbridge, Virginia 22195
Email: fabevidence@gmail.com

No part of this book may be reproduced in any form or by any means including electronic, mechanical or photocopying or stored in a retrieval system without permission in writing from the publisher except by a reviewer who may quote brief passages to be included in a review.

ISBN: 978-0-9860909-1-2

Manufactured and Printed in the United States of America

If you purchased this book without a cover, you should be aware that this book is stolen property. It is reported as "unsold and destroyed" to the publisher, and neither the author nor the publisher has received any payment for this "stripped" book.

Dedication

To law enforcement personnel fired or falsely imprisoned by deliberate, fabricated evidence.

TABLE OF CONTENTS

Preface 7

Introduction 11

Chapter 1: Marion/Walthall Correctional Facility 15

Chapter 2: Marion County Sheriff's Department 26

Chapter 3: Mississippi Department of Corrections 48

Chapter 4: Office of the Attorney General 66

Chapter 5: Termination 100

Chapter 6: Equal Employment Opportunity
   Commission's Charge of Discrimination 118

Chapter 7: Britton Mosley, Sr., *versus* Marion
   County Sheriff's Department 136

Chapter 8: Mississippi State Conference of the
   NAACP's Investigation 157

Chapter 9: Congressional Inquiry 176

Chapter 10: Mississippi Department of Corruption 186

Conclusion 199

About the Authors 207

PREFACE

According to The International Centre for Prison Studies (www.prisonstudies.org), the United States of America holds the highest incarcerated rate in the world. This is partially due to the broken criminal justice system in the United States, where thousands of innocent people (accused individuals) are entering into plea deals for crimes they did not commit. For fear of receiving longer prison sentences, the innocent, but accused victims of the law, will agree with prosecutors in exchange for plea deals, based on fabricated evidence.

According to figures released by the Bureau of Justice Statistics (BJS), in 2013, 1.57 million Americans served prison sentences in state or federal penitentiaries, a slight decrease from nearly 1.6 million in 2011. According to the BJS report, *"Prisoners in 2012," for every 100,000 Americans, an estimated 480 people were serving at least a one-year sentence in a state prison during the year. In some states, the rate of incarceration was much higher. Louisiana, the state* with the highest rate, sentenced 893 people to a state prison for every 100,000 residents."

The state of Mississippi, historically known for unjust and wrongful incarceration of African Americans for nonviolent offenses, maintains its rank as the second highest in the United States, with 717 sentenced prisoners per 100,000 residents as of 2012. Even as the prison population declined across the country, it increased in Mississippi. Between 2011 and 2012, according to BSJ, it grew 4.1%, a faster rate of growth than all but two other states. Although the $41.51 daily cost to house an inmate in Mississippi is well below the national average of $65.41, the state's corrections system is still $30 million in the hole for the 2013 fiscal year. Much of that is due to inmate growth.

According to the Mississippi Corrections and Criminal Justice Task Force's 2013 Final Report, *"An independent analysis of Mississippi Department of Corrections' data revealed that nearly three-quarters of individuals admitted to prison in FY2012 were sentenced for nonviolent crimes. Between FY2002 and FY2012, the number of nonviolent offenders admitted to prison rose 33 percent. This growing population of nonviolent offenders is also staying longer: newly sentenced nonviolent prisoners released in FY2012 stayed in prison an average of 10.5 percent longer than those released 10 years before. For some nonviolent offense types, this growth in length of stay was even more pronounced: length of prison stay for drug possession offenders, for example, rose 31 percent from FY2002 to FY2012."*

In early 2000, the Mississippi Legislature authorized 15 additional county/regional facilities. These additional facilities were all under the leadership of former Deputy Commissioner Chris Epps, who pled guilty to corruption charges in November 2015, monitored the operation of these facilities. The criminal justice system in Mississippi has built an entire economy around state and county/regional facilities. These facilities no longer seem to be an institution of rehabilitation, but rather a monopoly for earning revenue from "mass incarceration."

INTRODUCTION

Fabricating Evidence II: Office of the Attorney General/ Mississippi Department of Corrections Integrity Meltdown is the sequel to *Fabricating Evidence: Drug Set-up/Cover-Up of a Correctional Whistleblower* that exposed illegal activities within the Mississippi Department of Corrections. In this book, we will show how staff members within the Mississippi Department of Corrections and Marion County Sheriff's Department targeted prison officials within the Marion/Walthall Correctional Facility in Columbia, Mississippi. The unlawful actions by high-ranking state and county law enforcement officials are violations of federal and state laws due to the nature of the crimes committed through political, racial, and fabricated evidence that destroyed the reputation and careers of two law-abiding correctional employees: John "Jimmy" Fancher and Britton Mosley, Sr.

John "Jimmy" Fancher, of Irish decent, is a decorated United States Marine Vietnam Veteran who served his country from

1967 to 1973. After receiving an honorable discharge, in 1983, Jimmy entered the field of law enforcement as a corrections officer at the Mississippi State Penitentiary in Parchman, Mississippi. Upon a promotion and transfer to South Mississippi Correctional Institute in Leakesville, Mississippi, Jimmy worked as a captain until his appointment to Warden of the Marion/Walthall Corrections Facility. This position came to an unpleasant end after Marion County Sheriff "Rip" Stringer wrongfully terminated him. Fancher's wrongful termination was politically motivated to derail his career and wrongfully terminate based on fabricated evidence.

Britton Mosley, Sr., an African American and former industrial worker (shipbuilding), entered into the corrections field as a correctional officer at South Mississippi Correctional Institute, under the supervision of Captain John "Jimmy" Fancher. When Fancher was promoted to Warden of the Marion/Walthall Corrections Facility, he selected and promoted the seven-year corrections veteran, Mosley, to Captain/Assistant Chief of Security of the Marion/Walthall Corrections Facility.

Mosley and Fancher made exceptional sacrifices and achievements in administration. They scored the highest American Correctional Association grade in regional correctional facilities in

Mississippi, along with positively affecting the lives of thousands of incarcerated men. However, their impact was short-lived due to being falsely accused of fabricated crimes that were endorsed by corrupt, high-ranking state and local law enforcement officials. An intensive state investigation proved all allegations and wrongdoings to be untrue.

John "Jimmy" Fancher and Britton Mosley, Sr., were wrongfully terminated on the grounds of illegitimate political connections, racial discrimination, and retaliation. This book exclusively reveals the process that was taken, targeting Fancher and Mosley that dramatically affected their lives. The justice system in Mississippi is broken and corrupted.

Writing this book was a combination of pain and anger for Fancher and Mosley. However, the truth must be told.

CHAPTER 1

Marion/Walthall Correctional Facility

On March 2, 1999, Marion/Walthall Correctional Facility, located in Columbia, Mississippi, began its operation as a state regional prison facility that housed up to 250 Mississippi Department of Corrections inmates for a fee paid by the Mississippi Department of Corrections.

The Marion County Board of Supervisors, the Marion County Sheriff's Department, and the Mississippi Department of Corrections executed an agreement for the County and Sheriff to have the sole right to manage, control, operate, and direct the performance of the details, which are stated and agreed upon in the subject of the terms. However, the Mississippi Department of Corrections ultimately monitors and authorizes the overall operation of the regional facility. With the authorized approval of the former Commissioner of the Mississippi Department of Corrections, James Anderson granted Jimmy Fancher the position of Warden in December 1998. Britton Mosley, Sr., previously worked under the supervision of Jimmy Fancher for seven years as a correctional officer at the Mississippi Department of Corrections' South Mississippi Correctional Facility in Leakesville, Mississippi. With the official approval for Warden of the Marion/Walthall Corrections Facility, Jimmy Fancher properly approved James Harvey as his Deputy Warden and Britton Mosley, Sr., as Captain/Assistant Chief of Security in January 1999.

Upon arrival to the Marion/Walthall Corrections Facility, our primary duties were to initiate proper accommodations for the Marion/Walthall Corrections Facility to receive accreditation by the American Correctional Association to function under rightful standards as a correctional facility. In August 2000, the facility scored 99.7% on the American Correctional Association audit, which was the highest among county regional facilities in the state of Mississippi.

Fabricating Evidence II

RICHARD "Rip" STRINGER, Sheriff
Marion County
500 Courthouse Square, Suite 1
COLUMBIA, MS 39429
601-736-5051
December 14, 1998

Mr. James Anderson
Commissioner
Mississippi Department of Corrections
723 North President Street
Jackson, Mississippi, 39201

RE: Approval of Warden

Dear Commissioner Anderson,

    Construction is now underway on the Marion-Walthall Regional Correctional Facility in Marion County at Columbia. I know that the venture between Marion County and the Mississippi Department of Corrections will be a great asset to Marion County as well as the Mississippi Department of Corrections.

    The Inmate Housing Agreement between Marion County and the Mississippi Department of Corrections calls for your approval of the warden selected for the facility. I am submitting Mr. Jimmy Fancher to you for approval to be the warden for the facility. I feel that a man with his experience will do an excellent job in seeing that our facility is run professionally and effeciently. I want this facility to be a great success for all involved and I believe that a real key to that success will be the person selected as warden.

    I look forward to working with you and your agency in the future. If I or my office can ever assist you in any way, please call us. I look forward to your response concerning this request.

Sincerely,

Richard "Rip" Stringer

Richard "Rip" Stringer
Sheriff, Marion County, Mississippi

RWS:ir

STATE OF MISSISSIPPI
DEPARTMENT OF CORRECTIONS
JAMES V. ANDERSON
COMMISSIONER

John N. Grubbs
Deputy Commissioner

Institutional
(601)359-5618 • 5736 (FAX)

December 21, 1998

Mr. Lloyd Irvin Fortenberry, President
Marion County Board of Supervisors
250 Broad St., Suite 2
Columbia, MS 39429

RE: John Fancher

Dear Mr. Fortenberry:

Enclosed please find a copy of the approved request to employ Mr. John Fancher as warden of the Marion/Walthall County Regional Correctional Facility.

Sincerely,

John Grubbs

JNG/bds

Enc.

723 NORTH PRESIDENT STREET • JACKSON, MISSISSIPPI 39202
PHONE: (601)359-5600 • FAX: (601)359-5624

(3A)

Fabricating Evidence II

Marion County Board of Supervisors
250 Broad Street, Suite 2
COLUMBIA, MS 39429

FLOYD MOORE
DISTRICT 1

LLOYD I. FORTENBERRY
DISTRICT 2

JOHNNY GLEN STRINGER
DISTRICT 3

BILLY RAY McKENZIE
DISTRICT 4

CALVIN NEWSOM
DISTRICT 5

CASS BARNES
CLERK OF THE BOARD

December 10, 1998

Mr. John Grubbs
Deputy Commissioner of Institutions
Department of Corrections
723 North President Street
Jackson, Mississippi 39202

Re: Marion/Walthall County Regional Correctional Facility

Dear Mr. Grubbs:

This is to advise that the Sheriff and Board of Supervisors of Marion County, Mississippi, have considered several candidates for the job of warden of the captioned facility. Of those parties interviewed, the Sheriff and Board of Supervisors of Marion County, Mississippi, highly recommend Mr. John M. Fancher for the position of warden. The agreement between the Department of Corrections and Marion County, Mississippi, requires the approval of the Department of Corrections as to the employment of Mr. Fancher for this position. Therefore, at your earliest convenience, please advise if the Department of Corrections consents to the employment of Mr. Fancher as warden of the Marion/Walthall County Regional Correctional Facility. Your reply at the earliest possible date will be deeply appreciated.

With kindest regards, I am

Very truly yours,

MARION COUNTY BOARD OF SUPERVISORS

Joseph M. Shepard, Counsel

JMS/cl
C: Lloyd Irvin Fortenberry, President
Marion County Board of Supervisors
Mr. Rip Stringer, Sheriff
(F:\L.Files\L.-5483\L.ett.wpd)

STATE OF MISSISSIPPI
COUNTY OF MARION

I, the undersigned, Richard "Rip" Stringer, Sheriff of Marion County, Mississippi, do hereby appoint __JOHN M. FANCHER III__ to be a Deputy Sheriff of Marion County, Mississippi, and as such I hereby authorize him to do and perform all such acts as he may, can or ought to perform as such deputy, and this appointment is hereby submitted to the Board of Supervisors for approval in accordance with the statute in such cases made and provided.

WITNESS my signature this the __17__ day of __DECEMBER__, 199__8__.

Richard "Rip" Stringer
SHERIFF
MARION COUNTY, MISSISSIPPI

OATH OF OFFICE

I, __JOHN M. FANCHER III__, do solemnly swear that I will faithfully support the Constitution of the United States and the State of Mississippi, and obey the laws thereof; that I am not disqualified from holding the office of Deputy Sheriff of Marion County in said State; that I will faithfully discharge the duties of the office upon which I am about to enter. SO HELP ME GOD.

SWORN TO AND SUBSCRIBED before me, this the __17__ day of __DECEMBER__, 199__8__.

My Commission Expires __8-13-99__.

Fabricating Evidence II

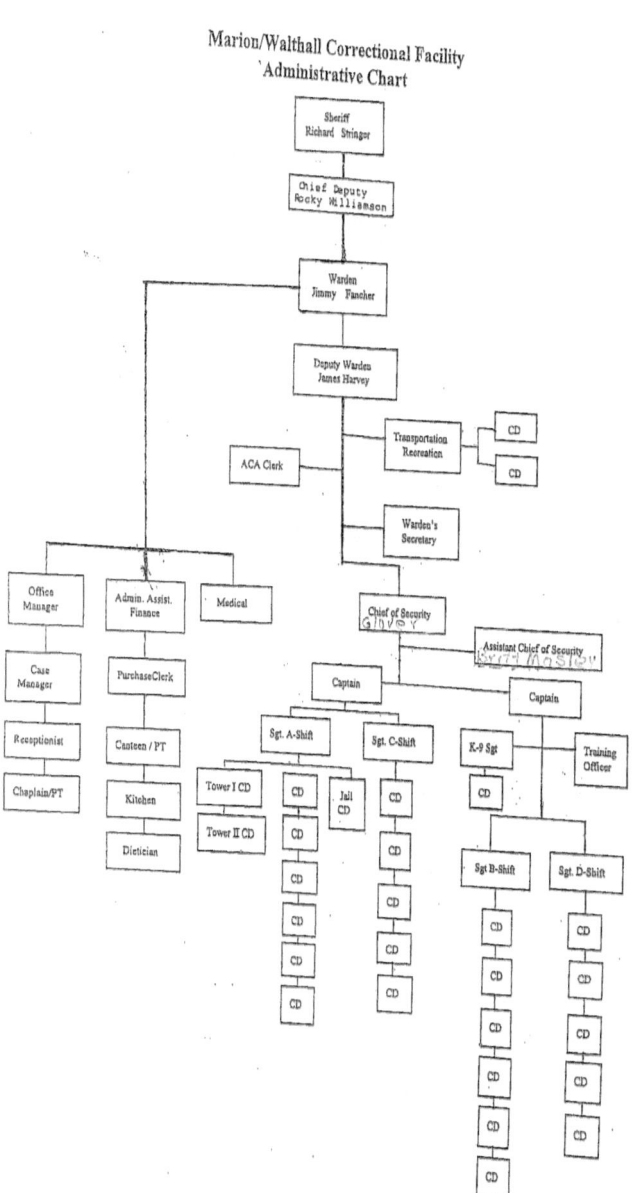

21

Britton Mosley, Sr. & John Fancher

RICHARD "RIP" STRINGER, Sheriff
JIMMY FANCHER, Warden
MARION/WALTHALL CORRECTIONAL FACILITY
503 South Main Street
Columbia, MS 39429

Phone
(601) 736-3621

Fax
(601) 736-4473

Monday, August 14, 2000

THIS LETTER OF COMMENDATION IS IN ACKNOWLEDGMENT OF THE OUTSTANDING JOB PERFORMED BY CAPTAIN __BRITTON MOSLEY__ IN PREPARATION FOR AND DURING THE RECENT A.C.A. AUDIT AT THE FACILITY.

MARION/WALTHALL CORRECTIONAL FACILITY SCORED 99.2%, WHICH IS THE HIGHEST AMONG COUNTY REGIONAL FACILITIES. I TRULY APPRECIATE YOUR EFFORTS AND DEDICATION.

SINCERELY,

Jimmy Fancher

JIMMY FANCHER, WARDEN

Fabricating Evidence II

American Correctional Association
and the
Commission on Accreditation for Corrections

COMPLIANCE TALLY

Manual Type	Adult Correctional Institutions, Third Edition
Facility/Program	MARION WALTHALL CORRECTIONAL FACILITY COL. MS
Audit Dates	AUGUST 7-9, 2000
Auditor(s)	FRED FREY, EUGENE RAY & GAIL LAFFERTY

Please check one:
- ● January 1998 Correctional Standards Supplement
- ○ January 1996 Correctional Standards Supplement
- ○ Other _____

	MANDATORY	NON-MANDATORY
Number of Standards in Manual	41	443
Number Not Applicable	0	30
Number Applicable	41	413
Number Non-Compliance	0	3
Number in Compliance	41	409
Percentage (%) of Compliance	100%	99.2%

- Number of Standards *minus* Number of Not Applicable *equals* Number Applicable
- Number Applicable *minus* Number Non-Compliance *equals* Number Compliance
- Number Compliance *divided by* Number Applicable *equals* Percentage of Compliance

American Correctional Association (ACA): Past, Present and Future

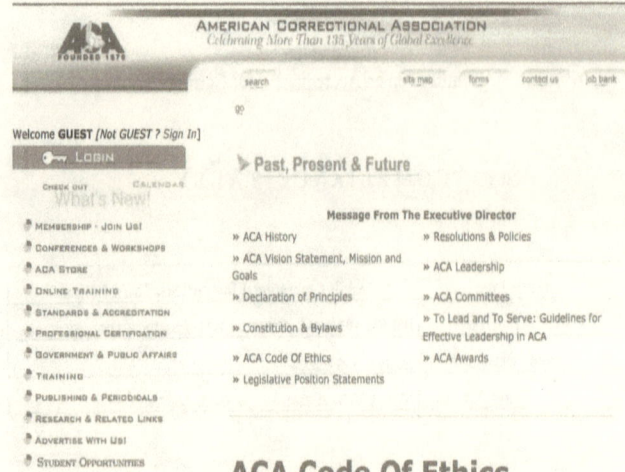

ACA Code Of Ethics

Preamble

The American Correctional Association expects of its members unfailing honesty, respect for the dignity and individuality of human beings and a commitment to professional and compassionate service. To this end, we subscribe to the following principles.

1. Members shall respect and protect the civil and legal rights of all individuals.

2. Members shall treat every professional situation with concern for the welfare of the individuals involved and with no intent to personal gain.

3. Members shall maintain relationships with colleagues to promote mutual respect within the profession and improve the quality of service.

4. Members shall make public criticism of their colleagues or their agencies only when warranted, verifiable, and constructive.

5. Members shall respect the importance of all disciplines within the criminal justice system and work to improve cooperation with each segment.

6. Members shall honor the public's right to information and share information with the public to the extent permitted by law subject to individuals' right to privacy.

7. Members shall respect and protect the right of the public to be safeguarded from criminal activity.

8. Members shall refrain from using their positions to secure personal privileges or advantages.

9. Members shall refrain from allowing personal interest to impair objectivity in the performance of duty while acting in an official capacity.

http://www.aca.org/pastpresentfuture/ethics.asp   3/11/2010

Fabricating Evidence II

American Correctional Association (ACA): Past, Present and Future

10. Members shall refrain from entering into any formal or informal activity or agreement which presents a conflict of interest or is inconsistent with the conscientious performance of duties.

11. Members shall refrain from accepting any gifts, services, or favors that is or appears to be improper or implies an obligation inconsistent with the free and objective exercise of professional duties.

12. Members shall clearly differentiate between personal views/statements and views/statements/positions made on behalf of the agency or Association.

13. Members shall report to appropriate authorities any corrupt or unethical behaviors in which there is sufficient evidence to justify review.

14. Members shall refrain from discriminating against any individual because of race, gender, creed, national origin, religious affiliation, age, disability, or any other type of prohibited discrimination.

15. Members shall preserve the integrity of private information; they shall refrain from seeking information on individuals beyond that which is necessary to implement responsibilities and perform their duties; members shall refrain from revealing nonpublic information unless expressly authorized to do so.

16. Members shall make all appointments, promotions, and dismissals in accordance with established civil servicerules, applicable contract agreements, and individual merit, rather than furtherance of personal interests.

17. Members shall respect, promote, and contribute to a work place that is safe, healthy, and free of harassment in any form.

Adopted by the Board of Governors and Delegate Assembly in August 1994.

American Correctional Association   206 N. Washington Street - Alexandria, VA 22314   Phone: (703) 224-0000 - Fax: (703) 224-0179

http://www.aca.org/pastpresentfuture/ethics.asp   3/11/2010

25

CHAPTER 2

Marion County Sheriff's Department

In April 2001, former Marion County Sheriff Richard "Rip" Stringer requested the Mississippi Attorney General's Office and Mississippi Department of Corrections to investigate Warden Jimmy Fancher, Deputy Warden James Harvey, and Captain Britton Mosley, Sr., on criminal and ethics violations, including illegal drug activity with inmates at the Marion/Walthall Corrections Facility. This ridiculous request by the Sheriff, in our opinion, was motivated by retaliation due to discrimination complaints, corrupt political involvement, and, most of all, the possibility of losing his position to Warden Jimmy Fancher, who began gaining notoriety within Marion County, and citizens wanted him to run for the upcoming sheriff election. The correctional officers that work at the Marion/Walthall Corrections Facility are deputies of the Sheriff's Department. Therefore, they are law enforcement officers.

Fabricating Evidence II

In January 2001, Captain Britton Mosley, Sr., filed an Equal Employment Opportunity Commission (EEOC) claim for discrimination against the Marion County Sheriff's Department after being promoted to Assistant Chief of Security because Chief Johnnie Glover did not possess the experience to do the job. When Johnnie Glover finished the Marion/Walthall Corrections Facility's in-house training academy, Mosley was one of the instructors. Sheriff Stringer promoted Mosley to be Chief Glover's assistant because he couldn't do the job. It is alleged that Glover was the Sheriff's cousin by marriage. Chief Glover's dislike for Mosley was well known throughout the Sheriff's Department. Mosley was subjected to verbal harassment, physical threats and an attempted conspiracy to plant drugs on Mosley's possession.

The drug set-up allegation almost became a reality. On August 12, 2000, Marion County Sheriff's Correctional Officer Marlene Warner was busted with two plastic bags of marijuana. It is alleged that Correctional Office Warner was never convicted of drug charges. Allegations were that the drugs were going to be used for the drug set-up plot.

There was an ongoing situation of racism and injustice between Sheriff Stringer, Major Glover, and staff members. There were complaints from families during visitation at the Marion/Walthall Corrections Facility. A white woman, who was to marry an African American inmate, filed a complaint. The complaint stated that Captain Chuck Abrams (a white man) told her, "We should stick to our own kind." Also, Captain Abrams and Chief Glover stared at the bi-racial family during the prisoner's visitation. In March 2001, Marion County Sheriff's deputies forcefully and inappropriately interrupted a family gathering at the Columbia Water Park, given by the African American fraternity Omega Psi Phi. This interruption by county law officials was on the terms of gang activity in effect by an alleged gang called the Q-Dogs, which is the common nickname of the fraternity members of Omega Psi Phi.

Sheriff Stringer refused to take any disciplinary actions against these employees. Mosley wasn't surprised, as he remembered a conversation he had with Fancher. "Watch your back," because Sheriff Stringer was a racist bigot.

There is a misconception in America that Mississippi has gotten rid of its racist past. Mosley was reluctant about working in law enforcement because of the tension between law enforcement and the African American community. This has been a painful experience.

Fabricating Evidence II

Former Warden Jimmy Fancher alleges that Sheriff Stringer supported the Department of Corrections Deputy Commissioner Chris Epps' retaliation against Fancher because Fancher was conducting an administrative investigation (ethics) on Sheriff Stringer's cousin, Johnnie Glover. This was one of many motives the Sheriff used to fire Jimmy Fancher, which ended his law enforcement career.

An inmate working odd jobs inside the Sheriff's office exposed an alleged plot against former Warden Jimmy Fancher, former Deputy Warden James Harvey, and former Captain Britton Mosley, Sr. The inmate overhead a conversation between Sheriff's deputies plotting to inflict bodily harm to the three law enforcement personnel. Allegations were to shoot Fancher at his home by plotting a fake robbery, shoot Harvey inside his house, and plant drugs inside the house, as if a drug deal had gone bad, and to shoot Mosley on his commute home during the night hours.

Historically, this type of terrorism was common with law enforcement personnel in Mississippi. African Americans are accustomed to this type of terrorism and violence legacy in Mississippi.

LORI LOWE, CSR 1230

Page 1

```
                 UNITED STATES DISTRICT COURT
                 SOUTHERN DISTRICT OF MISSISSIPPI
                       HATTIESBURG DIVISION

JAMES HARVEY, JR.                           PLAINTIFF
V                                           2:02CV121PG
RICHARD STRINGER, in his                    DEFENDANTS
Official Capacity as Sheriff of
Marion County, Mississippi,
and LLOYD FORTENBERRY,
President, Board of Supervisors,
Marion County, Mississippi


                    SHERIFF RICHARD STRINGER
                    Tuesday, December 16, 2003


APPEARANCES:

        Hiawatha Northington, II, Esq.
        Northington Law Firm
        P.O. Box 1003
        Jackson, MS 39215-1003
        (REPRESENTING THE PLAINTIFF)


        Kenneth B. Rector, Esq.
        Wheeless, Shappley, Bailess & Rector
        P.O. Box 991
        Vicksburg, MS 39181
        (REPRESENTING THE DEFENDANT, RICHARD STRINGER)


                     LORI LOWE, CSR 1230
             P.O. BOX 16972 - HATTIESBURG, MS 39304-6972
                (601) 264-5513 OR 736-6895 IN COLUMBIA
```

Page 2

The DEPOSITION OF SHERIFF RICHARD STRINGER, taken in the captioned cause, pending in the United States District Court, Southern District of Mississippi, Hattiesburg Division, before Lori Lowe, Court Reporter and Notary Public of the State of Mississippi, said examination being conducted after the witness had been sworn, at the Marion County Sheriff's Office, 500 Courthouse Square, Columbia, MS on Tuesday, December 16, 2003, at approximately 10:40 a.m., and was completed.

****

It is STIPULATED by and between counsel representing the parties that this deposition is taken pursuant to subpoena, and/or notice, and/or agreement for all purposes in accordance with the Federal Rules of Civil Procedure.

It is FURTHER STIPULATED that all objections are reserved until the time of the trial of the cause, except as to form of the question and responsiveness of the answer, which must be made at the time of the taking of the deposition.

IT IS FURTHER STIPULATED that reading and signing of the deposition by the deponent is waived.

Page 3

1 SHERIFF RICHARD STRINGER
2 CALLED AS A WITNESS, HAVING BEEN FIRST DULY SWORN,
3 DEPOSED AS FOLLOWS:
4
5 BY MR. NORTHINGTON:
6   Q. My name is Hiawatha Northington. I represent
7 the plaintiff in this matter styled Harvey versus
8 Marion County, Mississippi, et al.
9   MR. NORTHINGTON: I'd like to state for the
10 record that this deposition is being taken
11 pursuant to agreement; no formal notice has been
12 filed. However, we will be following the Rules of
13 Federal Civil Procedure with regard to objections
14 and reservation of any objections until the
15 deposition will be used as evidence or be entered
16 into evidence at trial of this matter, if that's
17 okay with counsel.
18   MR. RECTOR: That's agreed.
19   Q. I'm sure Mr. Rector has told you how these
20 depositions go. Have you ever given a deposition
21 before?
22   A. I have.
23   Q. So you're familiar with the question and
24 answer format. I'll do my best to make the questions
25 clear to you. If there's any time that you don't

Page 4

1 understand what I'm asking, please feel free to stop me
2 and ask me to rephrase, and I'll be glad to do that for
3 you. If you don't interrupt me or ask me to stop, I'll
4 assume you understood the question I've asked. Also,
5 do your best to give verbal responses so the court
6 reporter can make sure she gets those down into the
7 record so whoever gets the benefit of looking at this
8 later will have a clear record of what happened and
9 what transpired.
10   A. I will.
11   Q. State your complete name for the record,
12 please.
13   A. Richard W. Stringer. They call me Rip.
14   Q. What's your current address?
15   A. 1 Rip Lane, Sandy Hook, Mississippi, 39478.
16   Q. That's here in Marion County?
17   A. That is.
18   Q. What's your current job position?
19   A. Sheriff, Marion County.
20   Q. How long have you been sheriff of Marion
21 County?
22   A. 12 years.
23   Q. You were just re-elected; were you not?
24   A. Yes.
25   Q. What did you do before you were first elected

P.O. Box 16972 - Hattiesburg, MS 39404-6972
(601) 264-5513 or 736-6895 in Columbia

Fabricating Evidence II

LORI LOWE, CSR 1230

25

1 drug activity at the facility?
2 A. Not that I -- I never did tell them anything
3 that I'm aware of, other than I did tell them that he
4 had filed -- prior filed an EEOC thing. And I spoke to
5 my chief deputy on that and told him just not even mess
6 with it, let somebody else handle it or whatever. If
7 that's -- not even mess with the inmate that came back
8 telling him stuff, leave it alone. And, of course,
9 when all that was over with, that had done passed. But
10 I did let them know that he had filed that, and that
11 was in a file that he filed. But all that was cleared.
12 Q. At the time --
13 MR. RECTOR: To clarify the record, the
14 "that" you're talking about related to drugs.
15 A. That's in response to his question about
16 drugs, yes.
17 Q. Now, talking about that particular incident,
18 was there, at any time, any inmate or any other
19 employee of the facility that made a complaint or
20 suggested to you that Mr. Harvey had been involved in
21 illegal drug activity?
22 A. In talking to some of the inmates, they would
23 say that they were involved in drug activity and that
24 drugs was going on and that those were the only two
25 that was having anything to do with them.

26

1 Q. Harvey and Fancher?
2 A. Yes, sir.
3 Q. What about Britt Mosley?
4 A. They said that he was in a group with them.
5 Seemed like there was someone else they mentioned.
6 Q. We've got Mosley, Harvey, Fancher.
7 A. Seemed like they mentioned somebody else that
8 didn't work here anymore, but at one time he was
9 involved with the group, you know.
10 Q. Now, what was the nature of their -- the drug
11 involvement? Were they selling drugs or were they
12 having people bring drugs on the facility --
13 A. From what the inmates would tell me -- I'm
14 sorry I interrupted you.
15 Q. That's okay.
16 A. The inmates would say that certain inmates
17 was dealing in drugs and they were aware of it and they
18 let it go on.
19 Q. Okay. So it was a situation where Harvey,
20 Fancher, even maybe Mr. Mosley, were aware that these
21 inmates were involved in this activity, and they were
22 observing it and didn't do anything about it?
23 A. Correct.
24 Q. It never was a situation where they alleged
25 that Mosley, Harvey, or Fancher sold drugs to the

27

1 inmates or bought drugs to the inmates to use or sell?
2 A. In talking to people, a lot of times they'll
3 stretch or say this or say that, but when you pinned
4 them down, they would say, well, apparently something
5 is going on because this inmate is doing it, and they
6 know it, and then they'll be called up and talked to,
7 and then they'll go back. They would reflect that they
8 were -- or did know what was going on because they
9 would meet with them on a regular basis, you know. But
10 as far as proof and that they were charged with it, no.
11 But if they were and could catch them, I would charge
12 them.
13 Q. But it never was a situation where it came to
14 that?
15 A. Never charged them.
16 Q. Other than the investigation you requested
17 from the attorney general's office, was there ever a
18 time that you requested anyone within the sheriff's
19 department of Marion County or employee of the
20 Marion-Walthall Correctional Facility to investigate
21 complaints against Harvey or Mosley or Fancher?
22 A. Not that I can recall as far as those, you
23 know, complaints on them. Something might have
24 happened inside the facility or, you know, in the other
25 side over there, the county side, that I would say,

28

1 well, we'll just get an investigator to look into it,
2 one of ours, check on it, where a complaint may have
3 been filed against an officer or something. But I
4 don't remember anything personally against them. Of
5 course, there may have been, but I can't remember it
6 right off.
7 Q. Now, I may be skipping around a little bit.
8 We talked briefly about the EEOC complaint that Mr.
9 Harvey had filed that was done away with or dismissed
10 regarding illegal drug use. Now, was there another
11 complaint filed by Mr. Mosley around that same time
12 surrounding that same allegation?
13 A. Could have been. I don't know.
14 Q. Okay.
15 A. I want to say he filed something.
16 Q. Did you have any conversations with Mr.
17 Harvey regarding that particular EEOC complaint that
18 was filed?
19 A. The only conversation I had with him was he
20 came to see me at my office with a briefcase and all,
21 and he came to see me to explain himself to me, what he
22 had done. And I -- I listened to what he had to say
23 and told him that any time he had a problem or if he
24 thought something was a problem, my door was open to
25 him or anyone else, come talk to me freely any time,

P.O. Box 16972 - Hattiesburg, MS 39404-6972
(601) 264-5513 or 736-6895 in Columbia

| ☐ Parchman MWCF | ☐ CMCF | ☐ SMCI | ☐ CWC |

INCIDENT REPORT

Page 1 of 1 Pages

FILE TITLE: SECURITY OPERATIONS   CASE STATUS:

BY: CAPT. BRITTON MOSLEY

AT MWCF

DATE 09-12-00

WITNESS(ES)

RELATED FILES:
⊗ Master
⊗ Security
⊗ C. Williamson
⊗ Warden
⊗ Employee Files

REPORT RE: INCIDENT WITH OFFICER MARLENE WARNER, CONTRABAND WAS FOUND.

ON TUESDAY AUGUST 12, 2000, AT APPROXIMATELY 1805 HRS. I, CAPT. BRITTON MOSLEY CONDUCTED A ROUTINE SECURITY CHECK OF OFFICER MARLENE WARNER'S PERSONAL PROPERTY. THIS WRITER CONDUCTED THE SEARCH OF OFFICER WARNER'S PROPERTY INSIDE OF DEPUTY WARDEN JAMES HARVEY'S OFFICE. DEPUTY WARDEN HARVEY AND OFFICER WARNER WAS PRESENT DURING THE SEARCH. UPON SEARCHING A PAIR OF BLACK COMBAT BOOTS BELONGING TO OFFICER WARNER, THIS WRITER FOUND TWO (2) PLASTIC ZIPLOC BAGS, EACH BAG CONTAINED AN UNDETERMINED AMOUNT OF WHAT APPEARED TO BE MARIJUANA. ALSO FOUND INSIDE OF THE BOOTS WERE TWO (2) PACKS OF BUGLER SMOKING TOBBACCO. DEPUTY WARDEN HARVEY ASK OFFICER WARNER TO BE SEATED AND HE NOTIFIED WARDEN JIMMY FANCHER OF THE SITUATION.
************************************END OF REPORT************************************

*John Moses (WR) was Warner's super —
he was not investigated.*

SIGNATURE OF OFFICER	APPROVED NAME TITLE	DATE
Britt Mosley	Deputy Warden Harvey	9-12-00

Controversy brews over warden firings

■ Ex-Marion-Walthall officials say politics, race behind sheriff's decision

The Associated Press

A battle over control of the Marion-Walthall Correctional Facility is brewing after the sheriff fired the warden and assistant warden — a move the two men say was based on politics and race.

Warden Jimmy Fancher and Assistant Warden James Harvey were fired by Marion County Sheriff Richard "Rip" Stringer last month in a letter, in which Stringer cited "the best interests" of the facility.

Fancher says his firing is political payback stemming from his testimony earlier this year before House and Senate corrections committees that the Department of Corrections was inflating prisoner cost numbers.

Fancher has said that county regional prisons are more efficient than state-run facilities.

The former warden alleges the sheriff supported the DOC because Fancher had investigated the sheriff's cousin for ethics breaches.

"Stringer said he had allegations made by me toward the staff and citizens of the county, but to this day I have not seen any allegations or reports," Fancher said.

Fancher's contract with the county says that the warden may be dismissed for "reasonable cause."

Repeated attempts to contact Stringer were unsuccessful.

The DOC is working in conjunction with the attorney general's office in an investigation of the Marion-Walthall facility, said Chris Epps, the DOC deputy commissioner of institutions.

Epps said he didn't know who or what is being investigated.

The DOC, Epps said, must approve the hiring of wardens, but it does not have to approve their firing.

Harvey, who is black, says he was fired because of his race.

"I was a black man who focused strictly on doing my job and following procedure," Harvey said. "The Marion County Sheriff's Department is not a procedure-oriented organization. They want to continue to do things in the good ol' boy mentality."

Members of the state NAACP are to meet with Attorney General Mike Moore today concerning Harvey's dismissal, L.A. Warren of the NAACP said.

Stringer replaced Fancher with interim warden Joe Mingo, a black man. Harvey was replaced by Johnnie Glover, the sheriff's cousin by marriage.

Joseph M. Shepard, the attorney for the Marion County supervisors — a party to Fancher's contract with the county — says a contract between the Marion County facility and the DOC appears to conflict with the county contract.

"The (state) inmate housing agreement provides that the warden serves at the will and the pleasure of the sheriff," Shepard said. "And the sheriff could summarily dismiss the warden without consulting with the Board of Supervisors."

Fancher's attorney, John Reeves, said what matters is the contract between Sheriff Stringer, the county board and Fancher.

"If they're now saying the very contract they drew up is invalid, that calls into question a lot of things — such as motive," Reeves said. "Why would the very people that drew it up now say it's invalid? That's untenable."

(This is a transcription of a segment of a taped conversation between as yet two unidentified state investigators, possibly from the Attorney General's office and the Mississippi Department of Corrections. Also present was Major Johnnie Glover, chief of security at the Marion-Walthall Correctional Facility and an unidentified person.)

Unknown State Investigator: "You can tell' em I need to tell everybody that I talk to that this is a state investigation. I hope they know what they're doing, a state criminal investigation and if anybody talks about this they can be charged. So you know you tell whoever that you get. Say you believe Fancher's scared to death of Harvey, so you don't know whether he's got the picture of him fucking the goat or what."

Major Glover: "Well, I mean it's obvious, you can see it. Even the damn convicts. The warden hops you know like he's working for him. The officers at that prison over there, they don't even give a shit anymore. The Whites try to do your job . . ."

Unknown State Investigator: "The damn Blacks don't."

Unknown State Investigator: (Asked a question, unable to interpret.)

Major Glover: "I've heard it too, but I don't know."

Unknown State Investigator: "I've heard it. I've heard it on the streets."

Unknown State Investigator: "Where at, here?"

Unknown State Investigator: "Yeah!"

Major Glover: "I know Warner was a Vice Lord, she had the tattoos."

Unknown State Investigator: "She get off?"

Major Glover: "Yeah, that Marlene Warner that they arrested. And Harvey's the one that hired her."

Unknown State Investigator: "That's not out of the ordinary though for them."

Unidentified Voice: "Right."

Unknown State Investigator: "Because I mean you go to Parchman and just about every damn guard in Unit 29 is a gang banger. Cause that's where all the gang members are locked up is unit 29 and every damn one of them guards are. And they don't make it a . . . you know they'll tell ya."

Fabricating Evidence II

Unknown State Investigator: "That's ridiculous."

TRANSCRIPT

Interview with Major Johnny Glover.   Date: October 18, 2000
Present at this Interview: Warden Jimmy Fancher
                                Deputy Warden James Harvey
                                Chief-of Security Johnny Glover

WF: O.K. Johnny, what this is all about is that during the last few weeks/months there have been rumors running. So, what this does is put to bed rumors.
WF: All answers are subject to polygraph. O.K.
JG: O.K.
WF: Did you inform Captain Abrams about the NCIC on Evans?
JG: No, I did not.
WF: Did you discuss it with anybody?
JG: The sheriff.
WF: O.K.
JG: Because he was sitting there when the NCIC was run and he asked me about it.
WF: You didn't discuss it with nobody else? O.K.
JG: No.
WF: Are you familiar with the drug bust on Officer Warner?
JG: Acknowledgement.
WF: I know you were helping Doug (Barnes) with an investigation on that. Did you discuss that investigation with anyone outside of you and Doug (Barnes)?
JG: No.
WF: No one?
JG: Acknowledged no.
WF: Did you make a statement that other staff were involved with her involved selling dope here at the facility.
JG: No, I did not. I know who did but I did not do it.
WF: O.K.
WF: Does the dog at K-9 unit belong to MHP?
JG: The man told me it was.
WF: Who was that?
JG: Leon Burns with the Highway Patrol.
WF: O.K. Alright.
WF: You have told me the truth all the way through?
JG: Yes Sir.
WF: O.K.
WF: Who is the guy that can verify that it belongs to them?
JG: Leon Burns.
WF: Last Name?
JG: Burns. B-U-R-N-S.
WF: O.K.

Fabricating Evidence II

JG: Why? What is th deal with the dog?
WF: O.K. All I am doing is trying to clear things up Johnny.
JG: They called and asked me and and I called and asked you.
WF: I know that but see that for two or three week period.
JG: I have went to the man three times and told him to come and get the dog.
WF: O.K. Alright. Well thats all I had. Like I said, we are just putting rumors to bed. You know how the rumors have been running here.
JG: Yes.
WF: O.K. Well thats what we are putting to sleep now. We are in full rumor control. That concludes the interview.

_____
Warden Jimmy Fancher

_____
Deputy Warden James Harvey

Britton Mosley, Sr. & John Fancher

☐ Parchman   𝔐arion 𝔚althall ℭorrectional 𝔉acility   ☐ CWC
               ☐ CMCF   ☐ SMCI

INCIDENT REPORT   Page   of   Pages

FILE TITLE: SECURITY OPERATIONS   CASE STATUS:

BY: SGT DAUGHDRILL   WITNESS(ES)   RELATED FILES:
( )
AT MWCF   ( )
                                                                                    ( )
DATE MARCH 27, 2001   ( )

REPORT RE:

ON SATURDAY, MARCH 24, 2001 AT APPROXIMATELY 14:00 HRS I K-9 SGT TIMMY DAUGHDRILL WAS CALLED AT MY HOME BY OFFICER NIKITA COOLEY AND INFORMED THAT CHEIF OF SECURITY MAJOR JOHNNY GLOVER WANTED ME TO REPORT IMMEDIATELY TO THE SHERIFF'S OFFICE. I, THEN ASKED OFFICER COOLEY FOR MAJOR GLOVER'S CELL PHONE NUMBER TO FIND OUT MORE DETAILS. UPON CALLING MAJOR GLOVER, HE STATED TO ME THAT THERE WAS A SITUATION WHERE A GROUP OF "BLACKS" HE REFERRED TO AS BEING GANG AFFILIATED WERE GATHERING AT THE COLUMBIA WATER PARK. HE SAID, THE ALLEGED GANGS NAME THE Q-DOGS. AT THIS TIME, MAJOR GLOVER INSTRUCTED ME BRING "COBRA" THE ATTACK DOG WITH ME. I STATED TO HIM THAT I HAD "JAKE" THE SECOND ATTACK DOG WITH ME AT HOME. HE THAN STATED TO BRING "JAKE" AND PICK "COBRA" UP AND BRING THEM BOTH. BOTH THESE DOGS ARE HIGHLY TRAINED ATTACK DOGS AND ARE USED SOLELY FOR THE PURPOSE OF ATTACI HUMANS. AFTER RETRIEVING THE DOG FROM THE MARION-WALTHALL FACILITY, I SGT DAUGHDRILL PROCEEDED TO THE COLUMBIA WATER PARK AS INSTRUCTED. UPON ARRIVING I AWAITED MAJOR JOHNNY GLOVER WHO ARRIVED SHORTLY AFTERWARDS WITH CAPT. CHARLES ABRAMS AND CORRECTIONAL DEPUTY RAY PITTMAN IN THE FACILITY VAN. ALSO PRESENT WERE CDS DESTRY POOLE AND RYAN FREEMAN FROM MARION WALTHALL. I THEN ASKED MAJOR GLOVER, "WHAT WAS GOING ON AND HE STATED IT WAS POSSIBLE RIOT SITUATION". AT THIS, POINT I, SGT DAUGHDRILL OBSERVED A ATMOSPHERE WITH PEOPLE BARBECUING AND KIDS PLAYING AND LISTENING TO MUSIC. BASED ON MY TRAINING AND EXPERIENCE I FELT THAT ATTACK DOGS WERE TOTALLY UNJUSTIFIED IN THIS SITUATION. I, SGT DAUGHDRILL WAS AT THE COLUMBIA WATER PARK FROM 1430 HRS UNTIL 1800 HRS AND DURING THIS PERIOD I NOTICED NO VIOLENT OR HOSTILE ACTS THAT WOULD JUSTIFY US BEING THERE.
--------------------------------END OF REPORT--------------------------------

SIGNATURE OF OFFICER   APPROVED NAME TITLE   DATE

Fabricating Evidence II

Marion Walthall Correctional Facility

☐ Parchman   ☐ CMCF   ☐ SMCI   ☐ CWC

INCIDENT REPORT   Page 1 of 1 Pages

FILE TITLE: CASE STATUS:

SECURITY OPERATIONS

BY: CD CORRENTE   WITNESS(ES)   RELATED FILES:

AT MWCF   ( )
                                                   ( )
                                                   ( )
DATE 03-09-01   ( )
                                                   ( )

REPORT RE: RACIAL REMARKS BY CD MOREE

ON 03-09-01, CD MOREE STATED TO THIS WRITER THAT HE WOULD LIKE TO HAVE A MUD DIVER ON HIS WALL. HE CONTINUED THESE REMARKS BY SAYING "NIGGER" SEVERAL TIMES. CHEIF OF SECURITY J. GLOVER AND CD R. PITTMAN WERE ALSO PRESENT. THIS IS NOT FIRST INCIDENT IN WHICH CD J. MOREE HAS USED THESE SORT OF RACIAL REMARKS WHEN REFERING TO BLACK PEOPLE IN MY PRESENCE.

SIGNATURE OF OFFICER   APPROVED NAME TITLE   DATE
                                                            3/26/01

Britton Mosley, Sr. & John Fancher

Marion Walthall Correctional Facility

Memorandum

To: Deputy Warden James Harvey
From: ACA Clerk Sharon Fancher
Date: Tuesday, March 27, 2001
Subject: Comments made by Capt. Abrams

Deputy Warden Harvey,

On Monday March 26, 2001, I was typing an incident report for CD Gary Corrente concerning racial remarks made by CD John Moree. At this time, Capt. Charles Abrams leaned over my shoulder and asked me what the incident report was about. I responded that this was confidential and no one was to see it. He stated that it would go no further than him and I responded that I understood, however, this was confidential. He stated that he was asking because of what he had heard over the radio over the weekend.

A few moments later, I stepped outside of the front of the facility where Captain Abrams and CD Corrente were sitting at the picnic table. Capt. Abrams stated that Marion County Sheriff's Department Investigator Doug Barnes had stated over the radio to the Marion County Dispatcher on Saturday, "He had spoken to the head 'spear-chunker'." He also stated that the Dispatcher reponded by telling him to turn his radio to channel two (2). This was in reference to the situation that occurred at the Columbia Water Park on Saturday with the Fraternity Omega Psi Phi where Investigator Barnes had spoken to the President of the Fraternity.

sf/yo

Fabricating Evidence II

RICHARD "RIP" STRINGER, Sheriff
JIMMY FANCHER, Warden

MARION/WALTHALL CORRECTIONAL FACILITY
503 South Main Street
Columbia, MS 39429

Phone
(601) 736-3621

Fax
(601) 736-4473

To: Richard 'Rip' Stringer, Sheriff

From: Jimmy Fancher, Warden

Date: November 16, 2000

Re: Polygraph of Major Johnny Glover and Captain Charles Abrams

After interviewing both Major Johhny Glover and Captain Charles Abrams, it was found that there were inconsistencies in both their given statements. In an effort to close this investigation, as well as protect Marion County from possible EEOC actions, it is my opinion that a polygraph examination is necessary. This will ensure that MWCF and Marion County are attempting to gain closure in this investigation and will take appropriate disciplinary action, if necessary.

Sincerely,

Jimmy Fancher, Warden

Britton Mosley, Sr. & John Fancher

RICHARD "RIP" STRINGER, Sheriff
JIMMY FANCHER, Warden

MARION/WALTHALL CORRECTIONAL FACILITY
503 South Main Street
Columbia, MS 39429

Phone
(601) 736-3621

Fax
(601) 736-4473

To: Major Johnny Glover, Chief of Security

From: Warden Jimmy Fancher

Date: October 13, 2000

Re: Administrative Investigation

On October 18, 2000 at 1000 hours, please report to the Warden's Office at the Marion/Walthall Correctional Facility for an administrative interview. In the event you can not attend, proper documentation in the form of a doctor's confirmation of appointment and/or illness shall be required. Attendance at this administrative interview is mandatory. If you have any questions regarding this administrative interview or can not attend, please contact your immediate supervisor Deputy Warden James Harvey for further information or to provide necessary documentation to reschedule this administrative interview.

cc: Sheriff Richard 'Rip' Stringer
Members of the Marion County Board of Supervisor's
Personnel File
Master File

Fabricating Evidence II

RICHARD "RIP" STRINGER, Sheriff
JIMMY FANCHER, Warden

MARION/WALTHALL CORRECTIONAL FACILITY
503 South Main Street
Columbia, MS 39429

Phone
(601) 736-3621

Fax
(601) 736-4473

To: Major Johnny Glover

From: Warden Jimmy Fancher

Date: Dec. 07, 2000

Re: Polygraph Examination

On December 12, 2000 at 10:30 a.m., you have been scheduled for a polygraph examination. You will need to report to the Hattiesburg Police Department no later than 10:15 a.m. and request to speak to Lt. Schuber. This examination is in reference to the ongoing invesigation being conducted by myself at this facility. Please record your travel mileage to and from this examination for reimbursement purposes.

Warden Jimmy Fancher

Britton Mosley, Sr. & John Fancher

ARTICLE VI
EMPLOYEES

SECTION 6.1 County Employees. The County, the Sheriff and their employees are associated with the State and MDOC only for the purpose(s) and to the extent set forth in this Agreement. With respect to the performance of the services set out herein, the County and the Sheriff are and shall be independent and, subject to the terms of this Agreement, shall have the sole right to manage, control, operate and direct the performance of the details of its duties under this Agreement. The County's agents and employees shall not accrue leave, retirement, insurance, bonding, use of the State vehicles or any other benefit afforded to the employees of the State as a result of this Agreement but shall be employees of the County and serve at the will and pleasure of the Warden. The Warden shall serve at the will and pleasure of the Sheriff. The Sheriff, with the advise and consent of MDOC, may enter into an agreement with the Warden whereby the Warden will agree to supervise the operation of the Facility as an independent contractor and not as an employee of the Sheriff or County.

SECTION 6.2 Sheriff. The Sheriff, with the advice and consent of the County and MDOC, shall appoint a Warden to supervise the operation of the facility. In operating the facility the warden shall be responsible for carrying out the obligations of the Sheriff and the County as set forth in this agreement. MDOC may, at any time, evaluate the operation of the Facility and, if after an evaluation, it is determined the Warden is not operating the Facility to the satisfaction of MDOC, then MDOC may ask the Sheriff to replace the Warden in which case, the Sheriff shall replace the Warden. In the event that the Sheriff replaces the warden for whatever reason, the appointment of a new Warden will be on the advice and consent of the County and MDOC. In the event MDOC determines for good cause shown that the Sheriff and Warden are unable or unwilling to operate the facility, then in that event MDOC may designate a management company to conduct the day to day operations of the Facility in lieu of the Warden with the costs of engaging said management company to be paid by the County from the per diem per Inmate paid to the County by MDOC. If the Sheriff, and the County elects to contract for professional services, such services to be paid by the County, other than those services authorized by the act, the Sheriff and the County must obtain the consent of the MDOC prior to contracting for such services. MDOC shall not be responsible for payment, above the per diem per Inmate, of any professional services unless agreed to in advance.

SECTION 6.3 Personnel.

(a) The Sheriff or Warden shall provide professional personnel to deliver twenty-four (24) hour care and supervision to Inmates, as well as administrative and support service personnel for the overall operation of the Facility, in accordance with ACA standards. Prior to employment with the Sheriff, applicants shall be subjected to a thorough background check and shall comply with MDOC policy and procedures relating thereto. During employment, selected employees will be drug tested on a random basis pursuant to the County policy. At no time shall

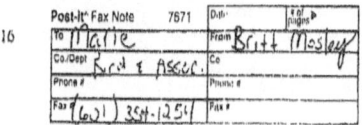

Fabricating Evidence II

IN WITNESS WHEREOF, the parties hereto have executed this Agreement as of the 27th day of August, 1997.

MISSISSIPPI DEPARTMENT OF CORRECTIONS ("MDOC")

By: S.W. Pickett
Commissioner of Corrections

ATTEST:
Deputy Commissioner of Corrections

MARION COUNTY, MISSISSIPPI ("the County")

By: Floyd Irvin Fortenberry
President, Board of Supervisors

ATTEST:
Cass Barnes
Clerk, Board of Supervisors

SHERIFF OF MARION COUNTY

By: Richard "Ric" Stringer
Sheriff, Marion County, Mississippi

Britton Mosley, Sr. & John Fancher

Letter to the editor
Terminations had no improper motives

As sheriff of Marion County, I am responsible under Mississippi law for the management of the Marion-Walthall Correctional Facility.

Also, under the terms of the contract between the Mississippi Department of Corrections and Marion County, I, as sheriff, have the responsibility for the operation of the facility. Of course, one man cannot perform all of the duties and responsibilities delegated to the Sheriff by law. Therefore, the law permits me to appoint deputies and to delegate some of my responsibilities to them.

Likewise, in the case of the Marion-Walthall Correctional Facility, the law authorizes me to appoint a warden, an assistant warden, and others to help carry out my responsibilities in connection with that operation.

By electing me sheriff, I understand that the people of Marion County expect and depend upon me to carry out all of the duties and obligations of my office diligently, honestly, fairly and to the best of my abilities. I have always attempted to undertake my obligations to the public in a serious and conscientious manner. I assure you that I will never knowingly be involved in any activity that is illegal or that could be construed to be even a technical violation of the law, and I expect the same commitment from each of my employees. I hold my employees to the same standard of conduct as I impose upon myself. Therefore, when I delegate any of the duties entrusted to me to deputies or other persons, I do so only after careful consideration. I expect all of my deputies and others who are charged with helping carry out any of my responsibilities as Sheriff to do so properly and effectively. I expect all of my employees to be solely dedicated to serving the public.

Over the last several months, I have deemed it necessary to terminate the employment of several employees of the correctional facility.

It is never easy to end someone's employment, and I did so only after serious consideration.

It was recently reported in The Columbian-Progress that the attorney general's office also investigated these employees.

The attorney general has elected not to pursue criminal charges against any former employee, believing that such matters should be dealt with by me administratively as their employer.

I agreed with this conclusion. I hope that all of the citizens of Marion County understand that I am not permitted to respond or publicly discuss all the details of these personnel matters in the newspaper or other media. Furthermore, at least one of these employees has sued Marion County. I know you will agree that trial of the case in the media is not in the best interest of the taxpayers of Marion County. However I can assure you that these terminations were not the result of any discrimination or other improper motive. In my entire tenure as sheriff of Marion County, I have diligently attempted to treat all of my employees fairly, equally and with respect regardless of their race, religion, sex or age. All employees' constitutional rights are protected to the best of my ability.

Thank you for trusting me to be your sheriff.

You have my solemn promise that all actions I take on your behalf, even those that I must keep confidential, are done to promote the best interests of the citizens of Marion County.

**Richard "Rip" Stringer
Marion County Sheriff**

New women's facility underway

A groundbreaking ceremony was held last week for a new women's facility which will be built next to the Marion-Walthall Correctional Facility.

The 13,000 square foot facility will house up to about 120 women. Only men are housed in the current correctional facility.

The new women's building, which will be about half the size of the existing men's facility, will be located next to the current building, but will be a separate facility.

The building, designed by the same architectural firm that designed the men's facility, will have a front entry similar to the front of the entrance on the state side of the existing building.

Sheriff Richard "Rip" Stringer said women inmates, who are currently housed in the old Marion County Jail, will be moved to the new facility once it opens. The new women's facility will consist of four dorms, housing 28 women per dorm. There is a possibility that one of the dorms may be used as a restitution center, Stringer said.

The contract time for construction of the new facility is 300 calendar days, and officials hope to have the building open by March.

The existing men's facility opened in March of 1999, exactly a year after a ground-breaking ceremony was held on March 2, 1998. The facility holds male state inmates and long-term male county inmates.

Sheriff Richard 'Rip' Stringer, left, members of the Marion County Board of Supervisors and other local officials participated in ast week's ground-breaking ceremony for the new women's correctional facility.

CHAPTER 3

Mississippi Department of Corrections

Meanwhile, on a state level, the Mississippi Department of Corrections was undergoing a transition of state commissioners. James Anderson was no longer the Commissioner of the Mississippi Department of Corrections, as his term had ended. He was succeeded by Robert Johnson, who was the new commissioner appointed by Governor Ronnie Musgrove. The Mississippi Department of Corrections Commissioner Robert Johnson and Deputy Commissioner Chris Epps wanted to take over Marion/Walthall Correctional Facility's canteen operations. However, the Marion County Board of Supervisors opposed the Mississippi Department of Corrections' take over actions, which began an ongoing conflict between state and county officials.

On February 27, 2001, Warden Fancher received a phone call from Deputy Commissioner Chris Epps, advising him that Commissioner Robert Johnson was submitting a letter to

Marion County Sheriff Richard "Rip" Stringer regarding the removal of Jimmy Fancher from the position of Warden. Deputy Commissioner Epps also stated that the Mississippi Department of Corrections threatened to lower the number of state inmates that were housed at the Marion/Walthall Corrections Facility if he disallowed and refused the Mississippi Department of Corrections to operate the regional facility's canteen. On another note, while in an the Mississippi Department of Corrections meeting in Jackson, Mississippi, Jimmy Fancher stated that after refusing to accept a bribe from Deputy Commissioner Chris Epps, the Deputy Commissioner told him "it will be financially and personally beneficial to accept the Mississippi Department of Corrections' control over the canteen."

The next plan of action for Jimmy Fancher was to lobby against the Mississippi Department of Corrections' actions by contacting Bennett Malone, who was a member of the Mississippi State Representative Chairman of House Correction Committee, and the late Robert Gene "Bunky" Huggins, who was the Mississippi Senator/Chairman of Senate Correction Committee to pass a bill to prohibit the Mississippi Department of Corrections to have control over county regional facilities' canteens. The law was successfully passed, after which Warden Jimmy Fancher was targeted by high-ranking the Mississippi Department of Corrections' officials.

In September 2001, Warden Jimmy Fancher received a letter from Deputy Commissioner Chris Epps, dated September 21, 2001. The letter informed Fancher that the Mississippi Department of Corrections Division of Institutions has scheduled the Marion/Walthall Corrections Facility for a monitoring and assessment audit to be conducted from October 9, 2001 through October 12, 2001. This audit came one year after the Marion/Walthall Corrections Facility had scored 99.7% on the American Correctional Association audit, which was the highest among county regional facilities at that time. It's worth mentioning that none of the three Mississippi Department of Corrections' institutions had undergone the American Correctional Association audit process. Fancher and Mosley became very suspicious of the Mississippi Department of Corrections' 24-team member "Witch Hunt/Hit Team." After all, why was it needed? Red flags went up when Charles Baily, Warden of South Mississippi Correctional Institute was one of the team leaders, and shoplifter (see attachments). As expected, after the Mississippi Department of Corrections' witch-hunt audit, there were numerous violations by this team, most of which were approved by the ACA audit team one year prior. This whole operation was in retaliation against Warden Fancher for being a whistleblower. One month after the Mississippi Department of Corrections' audit, Marion County Sheriff Richard Stringer fired Warden Jimmy Fancher.

Warden says MDOC is playing numbers game

Jimmy Fancher, warden of the Marion/Walthall Regional Correctional Facility, said this week he believes the Mississippi Department of Corrections is playing a numbers game in an effort to renegotiate contracts with the regional facilities.

Fancher said people are being led to believe that the regional facilities operate at a higher cost than the state institutions, but that pinning down the actual cost of housing prisoners at the state-run facilities can be difficult.

Figures provided by the American Correctional Association show the daily cost of housing a prisoner at Parchman is $48.55, while the daily costs at the Rankin and Greene County facilities are $41.39 and $37.43 respectively, he said.

Corrections Commissioner Robert Johnson has put the cost at about $42 per day to house inmates in the general population at the state institutions, and attorney Ron Welch, appointed to represent state prisoners, has placed the cost at about $49.92 per prisoner per day.

A comparison of costs showing a per-day cost of $8.43 for state prisoners includes only the costs of food, clothing and medical attention, Fancher said. Including such other costs as administrative costs, programs and housing and visitation brings that total up to $36.89. Comparing those same costs gives a per-day cost of $27.89 for private institutions and $23.86 for the regional facilities.

The Marion/Walthall facility has a contract with the state to house 200 state inmates at a rate of $26.42 per prisoner per day, and has the capacity to house up to 250, Fancher said, adding, "We can run at (a minimum of)181 and remain solvent."

The Greene County facility, which came on-line in 1989, was designed to house 500 inmates and has housed around 1,100 in the past, Fancher said. Even with the addition of the regional facilities, Greene County has still housed around 750, he said. As of Monday, there were 201 inmates in the Marion/Walthall facility, Fancher said.

"It costs about $9,643.30 to house one inmate at Marion/Walthall per year," he said. Taking the difference between that cost and the cost of housing prisoners at the Greene County facility, Fancher said, "If they brought us up to 250, it would mean a $1 million savings to the state."

Not only are the regional facilities housing prisoners at a lower cost, Fancher said, but they are doing it while meeting higher standards than the state facilities. The regional facilities are contractually bound to meet ACA standards, while the state's institutions are not, he said.

Fancher said he especially objects to an editorial which ran recently in The Clarion-Ledger which called the regional facilities "cash cows."

"The Mississippi Department of Corrections is a professionally run operation that is fully capable of managing the operation of prisons — public and private — and the role of regional jail facilities within its purview without politicians twisting the pursestrings," that editorial said, in part.

"The Department of Corrections is going for a corporate takeover," Fancher said, noting that the regional facilities have signed contracts that the state must honor.

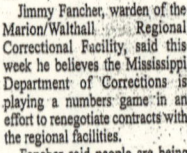

Fabricating Evidence II

Johnson: Using state over private prisons saves money

Robert Johnson   *10:35 a.m. CDT June 18, 2015*

(Photo: Thomas Beck)

At the end of this month, the Mississippi Department of Corrections Task Force — created by Gov. Bryant after the indictment of former MDOC Commissioner, and my successor, Chris Epps — is set to issue their recommendations regarding Mississippi's future with for-profit prisons.

I encourage them to recommend the state begin to phase out for-profit prisons and use the savings to (1) raise compensation for corrections officers to reduce corruption, (2) hire more qualified corrections officers to increase competency, (3) improve conditions in current facilities and (4) invest in proven rehabilitation and training programs.

Let me take you back about 20 years and tell you how we got here.

In the mid-to-late 1990's, Mississippi built 15 new prisons in seven years to address chronic overcrowding in our corrections system due to more stringent criminal and sentencing laws. The state relied on for-profit companies to come in and handle much of this expansion with the promise they would do so at a lower cost that saves taxpayer money. The deal was taxpayers would pay for the capital costs to build the new prison facilities and the private companies would operate them once completed.

In 2001, however, Mississippi faced another problem. After spending millions on building these new prisons, we had about 2,000 more prison beds than prisoners. Because for-profit prisons charged the state by the number of inmates they housed, it made more financial sense to me — as MDOC commissioner at the time — to put more prisoners in the state-run facilities that we were already paying for instead of paying an extra per diem to house them in a for-profit prison. It was like owning a hotel. Why would you pay to put somebody up in another hotel when you have an empty bed in your own? It was simple economics.

As you can imagine, this was not ideal for the companies operating the for-profit prisons, as they were losing money on empty beds the state was not paying for. So, they hired some lobbyists to convince legislators to establish a minimum bed quota for for-profit prison capacity, guaranteeing them both a certain number of prisoners and a statutory source of revenue.

This made no sense to me. Nor did it make sense to then-Gov. Ronnie Musgrove who vetoed legislation guaranteeing for profit prison companies a certain number of inmates. Unfortunately, his veto was ultimately overridden by the lobbyist-influenced Legislature.

Fast-forward about 15 years and the circumstances have not gotten any better. In fact, they are considerably worse now that these same companies are embroiled in the corruption scandal enveloping state government.

As of last month, the average occupancy in the four for-profit prisons that house the state's inmates was at 79 percent capacity. Meanwhile, the average occupancy in the three major state-run prisons was at 71 percent capacity. These state-run prisons have 3,360 empty beds, which is almost enough to hold the entire prison population housed in for-profit prisons. Again, if we have the space, why are we paying extra for them to stay in for-profit prisons?

It gets worse. These for-profit prisons are not keeping their promise to save the state money. In 2014, the average cost per day to keep an inmate at a for-profit prison was $53.52, including capital expenses to the taxpayer. The average cost per day to keep an inmate at one of the three major state-run prisons? $45.19 — over eight bucks cheaper per prisoner every day. If the 3,936 inmates in for-profit prisons were moved to these facilities today, it would save the state $32,786.88 tomorrow and nearly $12 million over the next year.

Britton Mosley, Sr. & John Fancher

A little over a month ago while speaking on a panel at Ole Miss, Andy Taggart — the co-chairman of the MDOC Task Force — claimed that he understands the argument that introducing for-profit prisons was "the only way to get the bed space we needed" 20 years ago, but that today, "it certainly seems like a bad idea." He went further to predict that for-profit prisons were not part of "the long-term future" of the Mississippi correction system.

I agree with him. There is an argument that for-profit prisons were necessary 20 years ago when Mississippi was desperate for a quick fix to our prison space problems. But now and for the foreseeable future, they are no longer necessary and are creating a financial burden on the taxpayers of Mississippi that is unsustainable.

As they finalize their recommendations in these last few weeks, I hope Mr. Taggart and the members of the MDOC Task Force take a hard look at both the history and the current facts and recommend Mississippi phase out its use of for-profit companies to run its prisons.

Robert Johnson was the Mississippi's corrections commissioner from 2000-2002, after previously serving as police chief, in Jackson, as well as Lansing and Jackson, Michigan. He is currently the owner of RL Johnson & Associates LLC.

Read or Share this story: http://on.thec-l.com/1Lhywzd

Former warden: Politics led to firing

On the anniversary of his firing, the former warden of the Marion/Walthall Regional Correctional Facility said he believes it was his attempt to thwart the state's attempt to encroach on the operation of the regional facilities — an action that was supported by county officials — that ultimately led to his removal.

"The ongoing fight between the department of Corrections and Marion County, Miss., continues," a letter from the attorney for the Marion County Board of Supervisors, dated Feb. 27, 2001, states. "Since beginning operations in March, 1999, the Marion/Walthall Regional Correctional Facility has filed a 'quarterly report' with the Department of Corrections...For several weeks, Chris Epps and Robert Johnson have insisted that all regional facilities file, additionally, a monthly report on a form which they have prescribed...So far, I have advised our warden to refuse to prepare and submit the new monthly report for I feel that if we give in to the Department of Corrections on any issue or request, they will continue their fight to take over operation of our facility."

The letter continues that, "Our warden, Jimmy Fancher, received a call from Chris Epps on the morning of Feb. 27, 2001, advising that Robert Johnson was about to submit a letter to the Marion County Sheriff demanding that Warden Fancher be removed. If such a letter is in fact received, Marion County wishes to respond by seeking an injunction and such other measures against the Department of Corrections as may be appropriate."

"I went to the sheriff and the board, and they said fight them," Fancher said of the state's encroachment on the regional facilities, such as the state's attempt to take over operation of the facilities' canteens.

Fancher said the Mississippi Department of Corrections threatened to cut the number of state prisoners housed at the regional facilities unless they agreed to allow MDOC to operate the canteens.

"I got a committee up involving all the county regionals. I got the wardens together," Fancher said.

At the time Fancher and Assistant Warden James Harvey were fired in October, 2001, Sheriff Richard "Rip" Stringer issued a press release that the decision to relieve the officers of their duties was "based on administrative problems inside the facility." Fancher countered, however, that the action was politically motivated.

Letters from two state agencies that investigated the regional facility state no wrongdoing was found on the part of Fancher.

"As you are aware, my office, along with the Department of Corrections conducted an investigation concerning alleged wrongdoing at the Marion/Walthall County Correctional Facility," a letter from the state Attorney General's office dated Jan. 16, 2002 states. "As a result of our investigation, there will be no criminal charges or ethics violations - pursued against either Fancher or Harvey."

A letter dated July 15, 2002 from the State Auditor's office states, "On 5/14/2001, the Office of the State Auditor received a complaint/referral against Jimmy Fancher, warden, alleging the following: Misuse of Public Funds...After a thorough investigation of the complaint and with legal advice from the OSA staff attorney and Office of the Attorney General, it was determined that the allegation against Jimmy Fancher, warden, could not be substantiated."

The letter continues that the case involving Fancher was closed on July 15, 2002.

A suit filed by Fancher claiming breach of contract had been set to be heard in September, but Hinds County Chancery Court Judge Stuart Robinson granted a motion for summary judgment, ruling that Fancher's contract was not valid because there was no record of it in the supervisors' minutes.

"This court has heard testimony and finds that political motivations likely played a significant role in the discharge of Fancher; however, this court is without the authority to address this issue as there is no valid contract in this case," Robinson's order states.

Britton Mosley, Sr. & John Fancher

STATE OF MISSISSIPPI
DEPARTMENT OF CORRECTIONS
ROBERT L. JOHNSON
COMMISSIONER

Christopher Epps
Deputy Commissioner

Institutions
(601) 359-5610 / 359-5323 (Fax)

September 12, 2001

Marion-Walthall Correctional Facility
Attention: Jimmy Fancher, Warden
503 South Main Street
Columbia, Mississippi 39429

Dear Warden Fancher:

The Mississippi Department of Corrections, Division of Institutions, has scheduled your facility for a Monitoring & Assessment Audit, to be conducted from October 9, 2001 through October 12th. I would appreciate your assistance in securing a location in your facility to accommodate approximately twenty-four (24) audit team members, starting at 3:00 p.m. on October 9, 2001. Please ensure you and your staff are available to assist and meet the team.

Mr. James Holman, Warden (Central Mississippi Correctional Facility), will be the Audit Team Coordinator for this meeting. We plan to complete this review by noon on Friday, October 12, 2001.

Should you have any questions, please do not hesitate to contact me at (601) 359-5607.

Sincerely,

Christopher Epps

pc: Mr. Robert L. Johnson, MDOC Commissioner
       Mr. Emmitt Sparkman, Superintendent – MSP
       Mr. Lawrence Kelly, Superintendent – CMCF
       Mr. C. David Turner, Superintendent – SMCI
       Mrs. Patricia Dean-Wilson, Bureau Director – Regional Facilities
       Mr. Justin Hall, Bureau Director – Private Facilities
       File

723 NORTH PRESIDENT STREET • JACKSON, MISSISSIPPI 39202-3097 • PHONE: (601) 359-5600
FAX: (601) 359-5624

Fabricating Evidence II

STATE OF MISSISSIPPI
DEPARTMENT OF CORRECTIONS
ROBERT L. JOHNSON
COMMISSIONER

Christopher Epps
Deputy Commissioner

Institutions
(601) 359-5610-5323 (F)

MEMORANDUM

DATE: September 11, 2001

TO: James Holman, Warden – CMCF (Site Audit Team Coordinator)
Charles Bailey, Warden – SMCI II
Aaron Jagers, Warden – EMCF
Smitty Jordan, ACA Accreditation Manager – CMCF
Gene Rowzee, Director of Food Services – MSP
Carole Kimble, Pre-Release Counselor – MSP
Anthony Cox, Unit Administrator – MSP
Ricky Moody, IAD – MSP
Willie Edwards, Compliance Officer – Central Office
Gay Marsalis, Special Projects Officer – Planning & Research
Glenn Spann, Special Projects Officer – Planning & Research
William "Bill" Hormann, Chief Fiscal Officer – SMCI
Dickie Wilkerson, IAD – SMCI
Dorothy Miller, Records Technician – SMCI
James Johnson, Deputy Warden – SMCI
Jesse Strittman, Fire & Safety Inspector – CMCF
Johnny Newsome, Case Manager – CMCF
Danny Jackson, Compliance Officer – MCCF
Charles Pickering, Compliance Officer – EMCF
Charlie Randall, Compliance Officer – WCCC
Lizar Polk, Delta Correctional Facility

FROM: Christopher Epps, Deputy Commissioner of Institutions

RE: MONITORING & ASSESSMENT TEAM AUDIT

I have scheduled the next above referenced audit at the Marion-Walthall County Correctional Facility at 503 South Main Street in Columbia, Mississippi (601) 736-3621. This audit will begin Tuesday, October 9, 2001 at 3:00 p.m. and end on Friday, October 12, 2001 at noon.

723 NORTH PRESIDENT STREET · JACKSON, MISSISSIPPI 39202
PHONE: (601)359-5600 · FAX: (601)359-5624

Audit Tool Assignments
Marion Walthall Co. Correctional Facility
October 9 – 12, 2001

Tool 1 — Administration/Information System/Research (Smitty Jordan & Charlie Randall)

Tool 2 — Fiscal Management (Willie Edwards)

Tool 3 — Personnel (William "Bill" Hormann)

Tool 4 — Training & Staff Development (Lizar Polk)

Tool 5 — Records/Reception/Orientation & Release (Dorothy Miller)

Tool 6 — Citizen Involvement and Volunteer & Religious Programs (Carol Kimble)

Tool 7 — Building & Safety Codes, Safety & Emergency Procedures, Sanitation & Hygiene (Jessie Strittman, Dickey Wilkerson & Charles Bailey)

Tool 8 — Earned Time & Classification, Rules & Discipline (Johnny Newsome)

Tool 9 — Security & Control (Aaron Jagers & Charles Pickering)

Tool 10 — Special Management (Anthony Cox)

Tool 11 — Inmate Rights (Glenn Spann)

Tool 12 — Food Services (Gene Rowzee)

Tool 13 — Health Care (Danny Jackson)

Tool 14 — Social Services & Academic, Vocational Education & Library/Recreation & Activities (Gay Marsalis)

Tool 15 — Work & Correctional Industries (James Johnson)

Tool 16 — Mail/Telephone/Visitation (Ricky Moody)

Fabricating Evidence II

STATE OF MISSISSIPPI
DEPARTMENT OF CORRECTIONS
ROBERT L. JOHNSON
COMMISSIONER

Lawrence Kelly, Superintendent
Central Mississippi Correctional Facility

Post Office Box 88550
Pearl, Mississippi 39208
(601) 932-2880

MARION-WALTHALL CO. CORRECTIONAL FACILITY
MONITORING AND ASSESSMENT

ITINERARY

TUESDAY, OCTOBER 9, 2001

1500 hours   Meet with team members

- Discuss Audit Process
- Discuss Audit Purpose
- Overview of Exit Briefing

1530 hours   Introduction of Staff

- Audit Team Members
- MWCCF Staff
- Review Audit Tool Assignment

1630 hours   Tour Facility

WEDNESDAY, OCTOBER 10, 2001

0900 hours   I. Audit Team Coordinator and Warden Discussion

- General Management
- Labor Law
- Employee Management Relations
- Criminal Justice System
- Relationship with other Agencies

723 NORTH PRESIDENT STREET•JACKSON, MISSISSIPPI 39202
PHONE: (601) 359-5600•FAX: (601) 359-5624

MARION-WALTHALL CO. CORRECTIONAL FACILITY
MONITORING AND ASSESSMENT – ITENERARY
PAGE 2

2. Audit Team Members and MWCCF Staff Visit Assigned Area/Monitor and Assess Procedures

(Wednesday, October 10, 2001 continued)

1200 hours	Lunch on your own
1300 hours	Continue Monitoring and Assessment
1630 hours	Progress Meeting

THURSDAY, OCTOBER 11, 2001

0900 hours	Continue Monitoring and Assessment
1200 hours	Lunch on your own
1300 hours	Progress Meeting
1400 hours	Continue Monitoring and Assessment

FRIDAY, OCTOBER 12, 2001

0900 hours	Submit Monitoring & Assessment Tools and Complete Training Forms
1000 hours	Exit Briefing

723 NORTH PRESIDENT STREET•JACKSON, MISSISSIPPI 39202
PHONE: (601) 359-5600•FAX: (601) 359-5624

Fabricating Evidence II

CONFIDENTIAL

INTEROFFICE MEMORANDUM

Internal Audit Division
723 North President Street
Jackson, MS 39202
359-5603

To: M. Gene Hill, Chief, I.A.D.

From: Johnny O. Covington, Integrity Investigator

Re: INVESTIGATION OF THE ARREST OF CHARLES A. BAILEY, CHIEF OF SECURITY, MDOC LEAKESVILLE, MISSISSIPPI; DOB: 8-6-59; SSN: 425-06-9336

Date: September 8, 1995

On 8-24-95, you directed I obtain all the information I could reference the alleged arrest of Bailey. Information had been provided to you that Bailey had been arrested in Pearl, Mississippi, on the charge of shoplifting from the Wal-Mart Store.

After contacting Bill Slade, Chief of Police, Pearl, Mississippi, he confirmed the arrest of Bailey. Chief Slade said Bailey was arrested on June 7, 1995, at 7:28 p.m. at the Wal-Mart Store for shoplifting (Pearl Police Department Case #95-6718770). After Chief Slade reviewed the arrest report, he advised me that Wal-Mart's Loss Prevention personnel had observed Bailey picking up items and concealing them in his pants and exiting the store without paying for them. (The items being two Uni-Ball Vision Roller Pens valued at $3.26, one Cellular Celltex Slimline Rechargeable Battery valued at $49.96; one Cellular Celltex Alkaline Battery Pack valued at $9.96, for a total of $63.18.) Bailey was apprehended by Wal-Mart Loss Prevention staff, and the Pearl Police Department was notified and responded. Bailey was released on his own recognizance and a court date set for 7-25-95 in Pearl, Mississippi City Court.

On 7-25-95, Bailey pled guilty and received a $358 fine with $150 being suspended and him paying $208. Bailey also received a 30-day sentence which was suspended. (Bailey was represented by Attorney Sam Wilkins, 555 Tombigbee Street, Jackson, Mississippi; phone number 601-354-0770.) Chief Slade informed me that an agreement between the City of Pearl and Charles A. Bailey for a Non-Adjudication Order had been signed.

MEMORANDUM - M. GENE HILL
RE: ARREST OF CHARLES A. BAILEY
SEPTEMBER 8, 1995
PAGE 2

Chief Slade provided the following copies for your review:

Item #1: Pearl Police Department Arrest Report

Item #2: Police Justice Affidavit signed by Wal-Mart employee, Keith Williams.

Item #3: Appearance Bond (agreement signed by Bailey to be released on his own recognizance).

Item #4: Wal-Mart Store, Inc., Loss Prevention Apprehension Report

Item #5: City of Pearl, Mississippi Adjudication Form.

On 8-29-95, I traveled to 2422 Old Brandon Road, Pearl, Mississippi; the office of the Municipal Court Clerk; phone number 932-3581. There I spoke with Clerk Merle McGee. Mrs. McGee informed me that when a Non-Adjudication Order is signed it would be forwarded to her, but as of 8-29-95, she has not received one for Charles A. Bailey and the July docket has not been printed (computer generated).

Mrs. McGee said she had been instructed by the Court that upon receipt of a Non-Adjudicated Order that the information on the subject should not be placed in the computer and if it was already in the system, the information should be deleted upon receipt of the order. In Mrs. McGee's opinion, a Non-Adjudication Order is a way to circumvent the legal system to expunge a person's arrest. Mrs. McGee supplied me with a copy of Charles A. Bailey's docket (abstract of court record) as of 8-29-95 (see attached labeled as Item #6).

James W. Shelton, Assistant City Prosecutor, City of Pearl, Mississippi; 210 St. Paul Street, Pearl, Mississippi; phone number: 601-939-7310; was interviewed to try and determine what a Non-Adjudication Order was; who issued it and how it was processed; and what timeframe it covered. Mr. Shelton's response was that a Non-Adjudication Order is the same as an Expulsion Order, but he could not go into enough detail to

MEMORANDUM - M. GENE HILL
RE: ARREST OF CHARLES A. BAILEY
SEPTEMBER 8, 1995
PAGE 3

answer my questions. He said he was not familiar enough with the statute to respond and if I would contact him on 8-30-95, he would supply me with the state statute which would explain a Non-Adjudication Order.

JOC:mev

Attachments (Items 1-6)

Britton Mosley, Sr. & John Fancher

47-5-931. Authorization for incarceration of ... offenders at county or regional correctional facility.

MISSISSIPPI CODE OF 1972
As Amended

SEC. 47-5-931. Authorization for incarceration of state offenders at county or regional correctional facility.

The Department of Corrections, in its discretion, may contract with the board of supervisors of one or more counties and/or with a regional facility jointly operated by two (2) or three (3) counties, to provide for housing, care and control of not more than two hundred fifty (250) offenders who are in the custody of the State of Mississippi. Any facility owned or leased by a county or counties for this purpose shall be designed, constructed, operated and maintained in accordance with American Correctional Association standards, and shall comply with all constitutional standards of the United States and the State of Mississippi, and with all court orders that may now or hereinafter be applicable to the facility. If the Department of Corrections contracts with more than one (1) county to house state offenders in county correctional facilities, excluding a regional facility, then the first of such facilities shall be constructed in Sharkey County and the second of such facilities shall be constructed in Jefferson County.

SOURCES: Laws, 1995, ch. 585, Sec. 1, eff from and after passage (approved April 7, 1995).

1997 Amendment:

SECTION 1. Section 47-5-931, Mississippi Code of 1972, is amended as follows:

47-5-931. (1) The Department of Corrections, in its discretion, may contract with the board of supervisors of one or more counties and/or with a regional facility jointly operated by two (2) or three (3) counties, to provide for housing, care and control of not more than two hundred fifty (250) offenders who are in the custody of the State of Mississippi. Any facility owned or leased by a county or counties for this purpose shall be designed, constructed, operated and maintained in accordance with American Correctional Association standards, and shall comply with all constitutional standards of the United States and the State of Mississippi, and with all court orders that may now or hereinafter be applicable to the facility. If the Department of Corrections contracts with more than one (1) county to house state offenders in county correctional facilities, excluding a regional facility, then the first of such facilities shall be constructed in Sharkey County and the second of such facilities shall be constructed in Jefferson County.

(2) The Department of Corrections shall contract with the boards of supervisors of the following counties to house state inmates in regional facilities: (a) Marion and Walthall Counties; (b) Carroll and Montgomery Counties; (c) Stone and Pearl River Counties; (d) Winston and Choctaw Counties; (e) Kemper and Noxubee Counties; (f) Holmes County and any contiguous county in which there is located an unapproved jail; and (g) Bolivar County and any contiguous county in which there is located an unapproved jail. The Department of Corrections shall decide the order of priority of the counties listed in this subsection with which it will contract for the housing of state inmates. For the purposes of this subsection the term "unapproved jail" means any jail that the local grand jury determines should be condemned or has found to be of substandard condition or is in need of substantial repair or reconstruction.

SOURCE: 1997 Laws, Chapter 457, Sec. 1, SB2879, Effective AP-March 25, 1997.

Chapter Index | Table of Contents

CHAPTER 4

Office of the Attorney General

At the request of former Marion County Sheriff Richard "Rip" Stringer, the Mississippi Office of the Attorney General, and the Mississippi Department of Corrections initiated a criminal investigation of Jimmy Fancher, Britton Mosley, Sr., and James Harvey in April 2001. At the time of this investigation, the Mississippi Attorney General was Michael "Mike" Moore. He, and his investigators, proceeded with the process for the state investigation.

In July 2001, during the course of the state investigation, an audio recording was made of a conversation between Attorney General Investigator Roger Cribbs, Marion County Sheriff Major Johnnie Glover, and alleged the Mississippi Department of Corrections Investigator Tom Wilson, in which they did not know they were being recorded. In the audio recording, Attorney General Investigator Roger Cribbs stated, "This is a state criminal investigation and if anyone talks about it, they will be charged." In the recording, Investigator Cribbs is clearly heard making explicit, sexual comments about Jimmy Fancher. Additionally, the entire group within the private investigation engaged in making racist comments about African Americans, in general. This type of conduct by the Attorney General, the Mississippi Department of Corrections, and Marion County Sheriff's employees violates federal and state laws. The Mississippi Department of Corrections' Policy Number 03.01 and the American Correctional Association Standard 3-4067, under "General Professional Conduct Code of Ethics" prohibit these types of actions by employees. The Attorney General of Mississippi is also the Chief Legal Officer of the state and the primary lawyer for the Mississippi Department of Corrections, in which Attorney General Mike Moore can be the only individual to prosecute or defend criminal misconduct of employees, and the investigation proceeded on to follow procedure.

After a nine-month investigation by the Office of the Attorney General and the Mississippi Department of Corrections, on January 18, 2002, an official conclusion to the Attorney General's investigation ordered by Sheriff Richard "Rip" Stringer. The report concluded that Jimmy Fancher, Britton Mosley, Sr., and James Harvey were exonerated of any wrongdoing, either criminally or ethically. Despite this, they were not offered their jobs back. The Office of the Attorney General, under the leadership of former Attorney General Mike Moore, has a history of racially and politically selective prosecutions. During President Bill Clinton's re-election in 1996, Mike Moore was a viable candidate for United States Attorney General.

During this era, President Clinton had declared a so-called "war on drugs." Law enforcement agencies were given federal funds to aggressively enforce these drug laws. Former Attorney General Mike Moore often accompanied law enforcement on drug raids and arrests. The only thing the so-called "war on drugs" achieved in Mississippi was filling up the state's prisons and ranking second highest in the nation in incarceration. In Mississippi, most of the people victimized by the failed "war on drugs" were African Americans. They were given extraordinarily long prison sentences for nonviolent, drug-related offenses. Mississippi incarcerates more people than developing countries, aided by the Office of the Attorney General. Evidence shows Special Assistant Attorney General Lee Martin's response to the criminal behavior committed by a white female nurse employed at the Marion/Walthall Corrections Facility, who was caught by a corrections officer on April 21, 2003 having sex with a state inmate in the facility's infirmary. The Marion County Sheriff's Office or the Office of the Attorney General brought no charges against the nurse. This act was a violation of state statue 97-3-97. However, an African-American female correctional officer at Central Mississippi Correctional Facility in Pearl, Mississippi, was arrested for allegedly having sex with an inmate. These types of selective prosecutions are racially and politically motivated, and are common in Mississippi. There's a great need for prison reform, and Mississippi needs to be ground zero for this movement.

It is worth mentioning that Attorney General Integrity Investigator Roger Cribb never interviewed former Warden Jimmy Fancher and former Deputy Warden James Harvey. The Office of the Attorney General conducted an intensive state criminal investigation at the Marion/Walthall Correctional Facility without interviewing the top two officials in charge of the facility. However, former Marion County Sheriff Richard "Rip" Stringer accused Fancher, Harvey, and Mosley of criminal and ethics violations.

Fabricating Evidence II

STATE OF MISSISSIPPI
OFFICE OF THE ATTORNEY GENERAL
PUBLIC INTEGRITY DIVISION

REPORT

CASE NO.:	02-0006W
SUBJECT:	Interview With Britton Mosley Sr.
DATE:	September 6, 2001
INVESTIGATOR:	Roger Cribb

Capt. Britton Mosley Sr.
Marion / Walthall Corr. Facility
Columbia, MS
Home Phone # 848-7447

On the above date, I interviewed Capt. Mosley at the Marion / Walthall Corr. Facility. Present during the interview was Capt. Mosley and myself. The interview was audio taped by myself and Capt. Mosley.

The purpose of this interview was to obtain information from Capt. Mosley concerning the investigation being conducted at the facility. Capt. Mosley said he came to work at the facility in 1999, and worked about 6 months. He said he left after that and went to work at the Isle Of Capri Casino.

Capt. Mosley said that he came back to work at Marion / Walthall in April of 2000, and has been there since. I asked Capt. Mosley about some of the allegations of illegal activities at the facility that had been reported to us.

Capt. Mosley said he was very familiar with the Warden and Asst. warden at the facility. He said that Jimmy Fancher was the Warden and James Harvey was the Asst. Warden.

I asked Mosley if he had ever seen any inmates doing any personal work for Fancher or Harvey. Mosley said he saw inmates Jeromy Stogner and another inmate working on Fancher and Harvey's boats. He said they painted and put new plywood in both boats. Mosley said he knows they purchased the materials for these jobs from Harry Taylors, because he helped them load the material.

Mosley said he also saw inmates build a box type deer stand for Harvey. He said he was told that inmate " Uncle Buck" made some rabbit cages for Chief Deputy Williamson, and was told the material came from the facility. He said he did not see this but was told this happened.

I asked Mosley if he had inmates do any personal work for him, and he said he had. He said he had inmate Freeman Conner tune his van and put valve cover gaskets on it. Mosley said he purchased the parts for this job from Auto Zone in Columbia.

Mosley said Sheriff Stringer took his lab dog to the K-9 unit at the facility to be housed and had Officer Tim Daudrill training the dog to retrieve ducks. Mosley said the dog was being fed food purchased by the facility. He said the county also paid a vet bill on the Sheriff's dog.

I asked Mosley if he knew about inmate Willie Brown selling steak, chicken, pork chops and fish plates out of the kitchen. Mosley said he heard about this after Brown was transferred from Marion County. He said he did not know about this prior to Brown leaving.

I asked Mosley about him being injured on the job at the facility. He said last year he got into a altercation with inmate Parker. He said Parker hit him in the mouth causing some of his teeth to be loosened. He said he had to go to the dentist and have work done on his teeth.

Mosley said he was off work from November 29, 2000, until February 2, 2001. He said Workmen Comp paid his medical bills, but he did not receive any other compensation from them. He said he received his regular salary from the County during the time he was off.

Mosley said he did not work anywhere while he was off injured, and after he came back to work, he did not take vacation.

Mosley said he surgery in April of this year, on both of his hands. He said he was off several weeks for this surgery.

Mosley said that Gail Dixon, Secretary at the Marion Walthall Corr. Facility, gave him a cell phone and told him that the type service he had on the phone was free nights and weekends. He said he used the phone for business only, but at nights and weekends he would make calls to his family, since he was told he had free nights and weekends.

He said later on, Warden Fancher came to him and told him he had a $ 400.00 phone bill. He said he found out that he did not have free nights and weekends. Mosley said he agreed to pay for his personal calls, but he has not paid the bill yet.

I asked Mosley about him staying in the camper trailer belonging to the County. He said during the time they were working on the ACA he was working a lot of hours and the Sheriff let him move one of the camper trailers the county owns onto the Corr. Facility property. He said Gail Dixon went to Wal-Mart and bought pots, pans, sheets etc. for the camper, and he stayed in it for several weeks. He said when he left the trailer, he took the pots, pans sheets, etc. to the K-9 unit.

WITNESS LIST

6055-MAJOR JOHNNIE GLOVER
6056-DEPUTY SHERIFF RICKIE BEARD
6057-PURCHASING CLERK GAIL DIXON
6058-PAYROLL CLERK CATHERINE "KITTEN" WILLIAMSON
6059-ASST. WARDEN JAMES HARVEY
6060-WARDEN JIMMY FANCHER
6061-INVESTIGATOR DOUG BARNES
6062-LAURA MCDANIEL
6063-GUARD RAY LYNN PITTMAN
6064-GUARD FNU MESSER
6065-COLUMBIA POLICE OFFICER HENRY SUMRALL
6066-CHIEF DEPUTY ROCKY WILLIAMSON
6067-DEPUTY DAVID MOREE
6068-GUARD LARRY LEWIS
6069-KITCHEN WORKER FNU/LNU "MUFFIN"
6070-KITCHEN WORKER RITA STATHAM

Fabricating Evidence II

1- A DEER STAND WAS BUILT FOR ASST. WARDEN HARVEY USING INMATE LABOR, LUMBER WAS ALLEGEDLY PURCHASED BY THE FACILITY. DEER STAND BEING A LARGE HOUSE TYPE STAND APPROX. 4X8 IN SIZE. TRANSPORTED AWAY FROM THE FACILITY BY GUARD TIMMY DAUGHDRILL. (6056,6055,6065,6066 & 6067)

2- WARDEN FANCHER HAD INMATES REDO HIS PERSONAL BOAT, IT WAS PAINTED AND THE MOTOR WAS WORKED ON. (6055 & 6065)

3- ASST. WARDEN HARVEY HAD INMATES REDO HIS PERSONAL BOAT, IT WAS PAINTED, PLYWOOD PLACED IN THE BOTTOM, AND PLYWOOD COVERED WITH CARPET. (6055 & 6065)

4- GUARD BRETT MOSELEY USED INMATE LABOR TO WORK ON HIS VAN, TUNE UP, REPLACE GASKETS, ETC. (6055)

5- CAPT. PAUL MCLENDON USED INMATE LABOR TO REBUILD THE MOTOR IN HIS FORD BRONCO. WARDEN FANCHER GAVE HIM PERMISSION TO DO SO AND ADVISED HIM TO DO IT AFTER DARK. (6055)

6- ASST. WARDEN HARVEY TAKES ITEMS OUT OF THE CANTEEN WITHOUT PAYING FOR THEM. (6057 &6062)

7- DIETICIAN JEANETTE DANIELS IS BRINGING FOOD ITEMS TO THE FACILITY WHICH IS BEING PREPARED IN THE PRISON KITCHEN AND SOLD TO INMATES. VEGETABLES ARE BEING USED WHICH ARE PURCHASED BY THE FACILITY. STEAK PLATES $5.00, PORK CHOP PLATES $2.50 & CHICKEN PLATES $3.50. (6063, 6064, 6056, 6070 & 6055)

8- GUARD BRETT MOSELEY RECEIVED A PAYCHECK FOR APPROX. 8-MONTHS AND WAS NOT WORKING. ASST. WARDEN HARVEY WOULD ALWAYS TAKE HIS CHECK, APPROX. TWO WEEKS AGO MOSELEY CAME BACK TO WORK HE WORKED ONE WEEK AND TOOK VACATION THE NEXT. ALLEGEDLY MOSELEY WAS WORKING AT THE STONE COUNTY CORRECTIONAL FACILITY AND A CASINO ON THE COAST DURING THE TIME LISTED ABOVE. (6055 & 6058)

9- GUARD CHARLES EVANS WAS GIVEN AN EXPENSE CHECK OCTOBER OF 2000 FOR THE AMOUNT OF $526 LISTED AS SCHOOLING EXPENSE, HE WAS ONLY IN A SCHOOL FOR APPORX. 2-DAYS. (6058)

10- GUARD CHARLES EVANS RECEIVED PAYCHECK WHILE NOT WORKING AT THE FACILITY. (6058)

MC 004

11-GUARD BRETT MOSELEY WAS ISSUED A CELL PHONE BY THE FACILITY, THE BILL WAS IN EXCESS OF $400.00 AFTER AN INVESTIGATION IT WAS FOUND THAT THE MAJORITY OF THE CALLS WERE LONG DISTANCE TO HIS RESIDENCE, THIS BILL HAS NOT BEEN PAID BY MOSELEY. (6061, 6057, 6058 & 6060)

12-WARDEN FANCHER'S DAUGHTER IS RECEIVING A FULL TIME PAYCHECK WHILE ATTENDING U.S.M. AS A FULL TIME STUDENT. SHE DID NOT WORK FOR SEVERAL WEEKS UPON BEGINNING SCHOOL, SHE NOW COMES TO WORK APPROX. TWO DAYS A WEEK. (6060, 6059 & 6058)

13-GUARD BRETT MOSELEY WAS LIVING IN A CAMPER TRAILER (OWNED BY THE SHERIFF'S OFFICE) ON THE GROUNDS OF THE FACILITY. WARDEN FANCHER SENT PURCHASING CLERK GAIL DIXON TO WALMART TO PURCHASE LINENS, COOKWARE, ETC. ALLEGEDLY WHEN MOSELEY MOVED OUT HE TOOK THE ITEMS PURCHASED BY THE FACILITY. (6060, 6059, 6057 & 6055)

14-INMATES WILL BE LOCKED DOWN FOR VIOLATIONS, ASST WARDEN HARVEY WILL TEAR UP THE PAPERWORK, RELEASE THEM FROM LOCKDOWN AND STATE THAT THE PAPERWORK WAS WRONG. (6055 & 6056)

15-WARDEN FANCHER HAS EVIDENCE IN HIS OFFICE, HAS NO CHAIN OF CUSTODY OR EVIDENCE LOG. A LARGE AMOUNT OF MARIJUANA WAS SEIZED BY AN OFFICER, UPON THIS OFFICER SEEING THE EVIDENCE AGAIN IN THE OFFICE OF THE WARDEN APPROX ½ WAS MISSING. (6055)

16-INMATES ARE PAYING FOR SPECIAL VISITS, $5.00 BEING PAID TO THE INMATE/TRUSTEE IN CHARGE OF THE LIST. CHIEF OF SECURITY JOHNNY GLOVER WAS IN CHARGE OF SPECIAL VISITS SEVERAL MONTHS AGO ASST WARDEN HARVEY TOOK THIS DUTY AWAY FROM GLOVER. (6055, 6056, & INMATE HORRIS BRANCH)

17-GUARD RHODA BARNES WAS ALLEGEDLY HAVING SEX WITH INMATES CHRIS BUCKHALTER, FNU PRESTON SIX-PACK AND AARON LNU UNDERGROUND. (6068)

18-GUARD RHODA BARNES AND GUARD PAM COOK ALLEGEDLY TOOK TWO INMATES OUT OF THE ZONE, AND PERFORMED ORAL SEX ON SAID INMATES. AN INMATE IN THE ZONE GOT MAD BECAUSE HE WAS NOT INVOLVED, SAID INMATE REPORTED IT TO ASST. WARDEN HARVEY. NO ACTION WAS TAKEN AGAINST THE GUARDS AND THE INMATES WERE TRANSFERRED. (6063 & 6058)

MC 005

19-GUARD MARLENE WARNER WAS CHARGED WITH DELIVERY OF A CONTROLLED SUBSTANCE, BY GUARD MOSELEY AND ASST. WARDEN HARVEY. WARNER WAS ALLEGEDLY SET-UP, WARNER CONFESSED TO HAVING SEX WITH INMATES FOR MONEY. (6061, 6055, 6069, 6060 & 6059)

Britton Mosley, Sr. & John Fancher

STATE OF MISSISSIPPI
OFFICE OF THE ATTORNEY GENERAL
PUBLIC INTEGRITY DIVISION

REPORT

CASE NO.:	02-0006W
SUBJECT:	Interview With Officer Destry Poole
DATE:	July 20, 2001
INVESTIGATOR:	Roger Cribb

Officer Destry Poole
27 E. Jackson Street
Foxworth, MS 39483
731-5164

On the above date, I interviewed Officer Poole in Columbia, MS in reference to the investigation on Marion / Walthall Correctional facility. Officer Poole is the transport and K-9 Officer for the facility, and has been employed there for 27 months.

Officer Poole says that there is a lot of corruption in the facility both with the inmates and employees. He said he saw inmate Jeromy Stogner building a large deer stand for Asst. Warden James Harvey last year. He does not know where the materials came from, but he said that the inmate was using the county equipment to build the stand.

Poole said that the deer stand was being built at the K-9 unit. He said that several other inmates helped with the deer stand but he can't remember who it was. Poole said it took several days to build the stand. He doesn't know how Harvey got the stand away from the facility.

Poole said he also saw inmate Ricky Potts work on Warden Fancher and Warden Harvey's boats. He said the inmate sanded the boats down and repainted them. Poole said that he also put new carpet and plywood in both boats. He doesn't know where the materials came from, but said the work was done at K-9 unit and the inmate was using county equipment to do the work. He said Payton Kendricks and Jeromy Stogner also helped on the boats.

Poole said that the inmates in the facility are making clocks, gun cabinets, and other items and are selling them outside the prison. He said the facility does not have a vo-

G:\USERS\RCRIB\DOCS\02-0006W\POOLE

Fabricating Evidence II

tech program. Poole said inmates are not allowed to have any money except on visiting days, and then they can only have up to $20.00 in quarters for canteen and that has to be spent on that day. Any other time, money is contraband.

Poole said that the Warden and Asst. Warden are corrupt and allow things to go on in the facility that are not right. He said Warden Fancher has gang members in the facility in key positions as trustees.

Poole said that Mrs. Jeanette Daniels is in charge of the kitchen, and has inmate Willie Brown working for her as a stock man. He said that on the weekends, Willie Brown cooks steaks, pork chops, chicken or fish and sells plates to the inmates. He said Mrs. Daniels knows about this, and allows this to happen. Poole does not know if Mrs. Daniels is getting any of the money from this operation or not.

Poole said that Brown sells the plates for around $5.00 each. Brown goes around and gets orders for the plates from the inmates and then he delivers them to the zones after he cooks them. He then collects the money from the inmates.

Poole said that Officer Britt Mosley who works at the facility was fired from Green County Facility for bringing drugs in the facility. He said this officer was involved in a scuffle with an inmate last year and had two teeth knocked out and has not worked in over 8 months, but he is being paid every pay day.

Poole said that female guards at the facility are having sex with the inmates. He said inmate Lonnie Harris saw guard Rhoda Barnes having sex with inmate Chris Buckhalter.

Poole said that when inmates do something wrong, the officers issue them RVR's but when the RVR's get to Fancher or Harvey they throw them away. Poole said that drugs are everywhere in the facility, and when they catch an inmate with drugs, Warden Harvey and Fancher will not do anything about it if the inmate involved is one of their friends.

Britton Mosley, Sr. & John Fancher

**STATE OF MISSISSIPPI
OFFICE OF THE ATTORNEY GENERAL
PUBLIC INTEGRITY DIVISION**

REPORT

CASE NO.:	02-0006W
SUBJECT:	Interview With Gail Dixon
DATE:	July 24, 2001
INVESTIGATOR:	Roger Cribb

Gail Dixon
Administrative Asst.
Marion / Walthall Corr. Facility
268 Sinclair Rd.
Columbia, MS 39429
744-0017

On the above date, I interviewed Gail Dixon, in Columbia, MS, in reference to the investigation on Marion / Walthall corr. Facility. Mrs. Dixon has been employed at the facility since February of 1999, and works in the Administrative Office.

Gail said that Jimmy Fancher is the Warden at the facility, and James Harvey is the Asst. Warden. She said both of them are corrupt, and allow things to happen at the facility that are not right.

Gail said that from May 16 to July 31 of 2000, Jimmy Fancher hired his daughter Sharon Fancher, under contract, to help with ACA work. She said after the July 31 Fancher hired her full time as the ACA Clerk to Warden James Harvey. Gail said that Sharon Fancher gets full benefits and is being paid $682.50 every two weeks. She is suppose to work five days per week, but is only working two days a week and goes to school at USM three days.

Gail said during deer season last year, Warden Harvey had inmates at the facility build him a deer stand. She said that several inmates were working on the deer stand, but the ones she knows were Kenny Sandifer, and James Lee. She said she saw these inmates working on the stand and they told her who it was for. She said the inmates were building the deer stand at K-9 unit. She does not know where the materials came from.

G:\USERS\RCRIB\DOCS\02-0006W\DIXON

MC 011

Fabricating Evidence II

Gail said that she also saw inmates working on Warden Fancher and Warden Harvey's boats at the K-9 unit. She said the sanded and painted both of the boats and replaced carpet and plywood in the boats. She does not know where the materials came from, but says the inmates painted the boats the same color of green that is used around the facility.

Gail said that Jeannette Daniels is the supervisor over the kitchen, and has one inmate working for her who is selling food to the inmates. She said the inmate is Willie Brown. She said he is selling steak, pork chops, chicken and fish plates on the weekends. She said the inmate cooks the food himself and normally does this on Sundays. She said that the facility does not serve pork chops, chicken, steak or fish.

Mrs. Dixon does not know how this food is getting in to the facility for the inmate to cook, but she does know that Mrs. Daniels knows about this and is allowing the inmate to do this. She said the inmate usually charges the other inmates $ 5.00 per plate.

Gail said that Doug Mason is the case manager for the facility, but he is never there. She said the facility has hired Benita Lott to do the case manager work, and is still paying Doug Mason $ 600.00 per month.

She said that officer Charles Evans went to Parchman to attend correctional officer school, but was kicked out for some reason. She said he charged the county for meals and mileage for the entire time he was suppose to be in school. She is not sure when he was kicked out.

She said this same officer went to some type of seminar in Georgia. He told Gail that he was going to learn how to write grants for Sheriff Stringer. She said Sheriff Stringer did not know anything about this.

Gail said that Officer Britt Mosley who works at the facility got in a altercation with a inmate and got hit in the mouth, and got two teeth knocked out. She said he has not worked in over 8 months but is still being paid.

STATE OF MISSISSIPPI
OFFICE OF THE ATTORNEY GENERAL
PUBLIC INTEGRITY DIVISION

REPORT

CASE NO.:	02-0006W
SUBJECT:	Interview With Officer Ray Lynn Pittman
DATE:	August 23, 2001
INVESTIGATOR:	Roger Cribb

Officer Ray Lynn Pittman
28 Stringer Loop Rd.
Foxworth, MS
736-8475

On the above date, I interviewed Officer Pittman in Columbia, MS. Present during this interview was Tom Wilson with the Department Of Corrections, Chief Deputy Rocky Williamson with the Marion County Sheriff's Office and myself.

Officer Pittman said he is employed with the Marion Walthall Corr. Facility as a part time Corr. Officer for 1 year and 6 months. He said he works 56 hours per pay period at the facility.

Pittman said that he knows Warden Fancher and Warden Harvey. He said the Wardens have gang members working in key positions as trustees at the facility. Pittman said that these gang members get by with anything they want to do because they are the warden's "boys".

Pittman said that inmates Tommy Redmond and Lonnie Harris told him they saw employees Rhoda Barnes and Pam Cook having oral sex with inmates Aaron Taylor and Chris Buckhalter in the medical facility at the prison.

Pittman said that the talk around the facility is that Pam Cook and Warden Harvey are having an affair.

Pittman said that he saw inmate Jeromy Stogner and some other inmates working on Warden Harvey and Warden Fancher's boats. He said they sanded and painted both boats and also replaced the plywood and carpet in the boats. He said this work was

G:\USERS\RCRIB\DOCS\02-0006W\PITTMAN

Fabricating Evidence II

being done at the K-9 unit at the facility. Pittman said that Officer Tim Daudrill picked up some of the materials used for the repair of these boats. Pittman said he thinks some of the materials came from Harry Taylors in Columbia.

Pittman said he also saw inmates building a large deer stand for Warden Harvey, and Tim Daudrill. He said some of the materials were purchased from Harry Taylors. He said inmates worked on the stands for about two months.

Officer Pittman gave the following accounts of other events he said he witnessed at the facility.

November 28, 2000 - He saw Warden Harvey let Rhoda Barnes, who was off-duty, in the front gate at the facility. She went to A Zone with a pair of shoes and a bag, and gave it to inmate known to him as "Sha Nay Nay".

January 23, 2001, 12:17 pm- Warden Harvey let Rhoda Barnes, who was off-duty, in front gate with package. Let her go in un-escorted and package not searched. She went to A Zone and dropped package off to an unknown inmate.

June 3, 2001, 2:45pm - Saw Jeanette Daniels bring in several bags of steaks, and give them to inmate Willie Brown. On this same day, he saw Willie Brown delivering plates of food to inmates in the zones.

June 23, 2001, around 4:30 pm- Pittman and Officer Destry Poole, saw Warden Harvey and employee Benita Lott engaged in some type of physical activity in her office.

June 28th 2001, 4:30 pm- Saw Jeanette Daniels bring in 3 large packs of pork chops, and gave them to Mrs. Franklin in the kitchen, and she gave them to Willie Brown. Warden Harvey let her in the gate.

G:\USERS\RCRIB\DOCS\02-0006\W\PITTMAN

MC 028

AFFIDAVIT

STATE OF MISSISSIPPI
COUNTY OF MARION

Personally appeared before me, the undersigned, RAY PITTMAN, who being by me first duly sworn on oath stated as follows:

1. I have personal knowledge of all the matters and things set forth in this affidavit.

2. I am employed as a correctional officer at the Marion Walthall Correctional Facility on a part-time basis. I also work part-time for the sheriff's department.

3. Many times an RVR would be prepared by a correctional officer which would simply disappear and never be processed. In one instance, an inmate actually made physical contact with a guard but the RVR was not processed by the warden.

4. I saw inmates working on boats belonging to Warden Fancher and Assistant Warden Harvey and I also saw inmates building a deer stand. The deer stand was being built at the time a new canine facility was being constructed at the facility.

5. Gennett Daniels, a kitchen employee, was involved in bringing food from outside the facility, preparing it at the facility, and selling it to inmates. Warden Fancher was aware of this and, in fact, I saw him let her in the gate on one occasion with packages of food. On another occasion, I counted over 50 plates being delivered into inmate zones.

6. Warden Fancher transferred into the correctional facility inmates that he knew at other facilities where he had worked. Many of these inmates were known gang members. Most of these people were given extensive privileges and authority throughout the prison. When the

Fabricating Evidence II

attorney general's office investigated the prison at the request of the sheriff, I participating in making a list of all of these gang members who had infiltrated the population at Fancher's request. All of the individuals on the list were transferred by the attorney general's office

5. Britton Mosley did not work at the facility for many months but remained on the payroll. Sharon Fancher, Jimmy Fancher's daughter, was hired supposedly to work as a case worker on legal matters but she never did any significant work. We could not find most of the paperwork that she was supposed to be working on when Mr. Fancher was terminated.

6. During the time Jimmy Fancher allowed Britton Mosley to live in the mobile office unit on the prison grounds, I would often see inmates going back and forth to the trailer in the small hours of the morning. This activity, of course, is strictly prohibited.

7. I advised the sheriff of all of the foregoing matters prior to the time that Mr. Fancher's employment was terminated.

RAY PITTMAN

SWORN TO and subscribed before me, this _____ day of _____, 2002.

Notary Public
My Commission Expires: _____

recorded during state investigation

Jason Straziuso
ASSOCIATED PRESS WRITER

JACKSON — An audio tape with racial profiling and a graphic sexual comment was secretly recorded during a state investigation into a Mississippi prison.

The state Attorney General's Office and the Mississippi Department of Corrections have been investigating the Marion-Walthall Correctional Facility since April. The tape allegedly was recorded during the probe, possibly July 20.

A copy of the audio tape was obtained and reviewed by The Associated Press.

The state NAACP has met with Attorney General Mike Moore and DOC officials about the recording. Both state agencies deny one of its investigators made an inappropriate remark.

The first voice on the tape — whose contents are scratchy and of varying quality — clearly says "this is a state investigation" and that "If anybody talks about this they can be charged."

A voice — which seems to be the same one — later makes a graphic sexual reference about the facility's former warden, Jimmy Fancher.

Another voice, which sounds different from the first, can be heard saying white prison workers at Marion-Walthall do their jobs, but "the damn blacks don't."

Lee Martin, an assistant attorney general, confirmed that an agency investigator was present during the conversation, but said the investigator did not make a racial comment.

Attorney general officials declined to name the investigator.

Martin said the racial statement also could not have been made by a DOC official because none was at the meeting.

The comments on the tape have created somewhat of an investigation within an investigation.

L.A. Warren, head of the legal redress division of the state NAACP, said his complaint to state officials centered on the racial comment, not the sexual one. He said another meeting between NAACP officials and Moore is scheduled in January to discuss the tape.

Two key questions remain unanswered: who made the comments, and who recorded the conversation.

Martin said there were four people in the room — an attorney general's investigator, two Marion County sheriff's deputies and a person being interviewed. None of the four is suspected of making the tape.

He said the AG's investigator does not remember who made the racial comments and that it was a matter for local officials to pursue.

Warren said the official explanation as to who was at the meeting has changed over time.

Warren says he was told by Martin in August that a DOC employee was present at the meeting. That DOC employee named by Martin no longer works for the agency, and Warren said he's since received conflicting information.

"The first time we met they should have known who was there. It should have been consistent from day one," Warren said.

"The only thing one can assume is that they have the facts and they're trying to cover them up."

Segments from tape

Selected segments of a conversation recorded while — according to Assistant Attorney General Lee Martin — one Attorney General investigator and two Marion County sheriff's deputies and a someone about allegations at the Marion-Walthall Correctional Facility.

A reference to "Fancher" is former warden Jimmy Fancher, who is white. A reference to "Harvey" is former assistant warden James Harvey, who is black. Both men have been fired for undisclosed violations.

The transcription was done by The Associated Press.

Voice 1: You can tell them that, and I need to tell everybody that I talk to, that this is a state investigation ... a state criminal investigation and if anybody talks about this you can be charged.

Conversation time elapses.

Voice 1: Boy you believe Fancher's scared to death of Harvey, so you don't know whether he's got the picture of him (sexual explative) a giost.

Voice 2: Well I mean it's obvious, you can see it. ... The warden hops, you know, like he's working for him, (time elapse) The officers at that prison, they don't even give a (explative) anymore. The whites try to do your job.

Voice 3: The damn blacks don't.

Conversation time elapses.

Another voice, unclear if some as those above: Because I mean you go to Parchman and just about every damn guard in unit 29 is a gang (unintelligible) cause that's where all the gang members are locked up is unit 29 and every damn one of them guards are.

— *The Associated Press*

Fabricating Evidence II

LOCAL/STATE

Online edition: www.hattiesburgamerican.com

Racist comments recorded in probe

Officials deny jail investigator was speaker on tape

JACKSON (AP) — An audio tape with racial profiling and a graphic sexual comment was secretly recorded during a state investigation into a Mississippi prison.

The state Attorney General's Office and the Mississippi Department of Corrections have been investigating the Marion-Walthall Correctional Facility since April. The tape allegedly was recorded during the probe, possibly July 20.

A copy of the audio tape was obtained and reviewed by The Associated Press.

The state NAACP has met with Attorney General Mike Moore and DOC officials about the recording. Both state agencies deny one of its investigators made an inappropriate remark.

The first voice on the tape — whose contents are scratchy and of varying quality — clearly says, "this is a state investigator" and that, "if anybody talks about this they can be charged."

A voice — which seems to be the same one — later makes a graphic sexual reference about the facility's former warden, Jimmy Fancher.

Another voice, which sounds different from the first, can be heard saying, white prison workers at Marion-Walthall do their jobs, but "the damn blacks don't."

Lee Martin, an assistant attorney general, confirmed that an agency investigator was present during the conversation, but said the investigator did not make a racial comment.

Attorney general officials declined to name the investigator.

Martin said the racial statement also could not have been made by a DOC official because none was at the meeting.

The comments on the tape have created somewhat of an investigation within an investigation.

L.A. Warren, head of the legal redress division of the state NAACP, said his complaint to state officials centered on the racial comment, not the sexual one. He said another meeting between NAACP officials and Moore is scheduled in January to discuss the tape.

Two key questions remain unanswered: who made the comments and who recorded the conversation.

Martin said there were four people in the room — an attorney general's investigator, two deputies and a person being interviewed. None of the four is suspected of making the tape.

He said the attorney general's investigator does not remember who made the racial comments and that it was a matter for local officials to pursue.

"One of (the deputies) will have to own up to whether they made the statement or not," Martin said. "I think it's an issue for the sheriff's department to deal with."

Warren said the official explanation as to who was at the Marion County sheriff deputies' meeting has changed over time.

Warren says he was told by Martin in August that a DOC employee was present at the meeting. That DOC employee no longer works for the agency, and Warren said he's since received conflicting information.

Racist comments recorded during investigation

By JASON STRAZIUSO
ASSOCIATED PRESS WRITER

JACKSON, Miss. (AP) — An audio tape with racial profiling and a graphic sexual comment was secretly recorded during a state investigation into a Mississippi prison.

The state Attorney General's Office and the Mississippi Department of Corrections have been investigating the Marion-Walthall Correctional Facility since April. The tape allegedly was recorded during the probe, possibly July 20.

A copy of the audio tape was obtained and reviewed by The Associated Press.

The state NAACP has met with Attorney General Mike Moore and DOC officials about the recording. Both state agencies deny one of its investigators made an inappropriate remark.

The first voice on the tape — whose contents are scratchy and of varying quality — clearly says "this is a state investigation" and that "if anybody talks about this they can be charged."

A voice — which seems to be the same one — later makes a graphic sexual reference about the facility's former warden, Jimmy Fancher.

Another voice, which sounds different from the first, can be heard saying white prison workers at Marion-Walthall do their jobs, but "the damn blacks don't."

Lee Martin, an assistant attorney general, confirmed that an agency investigator was present during the conversation, but said the investigator did not make a racial comment.

Attorney general officials declined to name the investigator.

Martin said the racial statement also could not have been made by a DOC official because none was at the meeting.

The comments on the tape have created somewhat of an investigation within an investigation.

L.A. Warren, head of the legal redress division of the state NAACP, said his complaint to state officials centered on the racial comment, not the sexual one. He said another meeting between NAACP officials and Moore is scheduled in January to discuss the tape.

Two key questions remain unanswered: who made the comments, and who recorded the conversation.

Martin said there were four people in the room — an attorney general's investigator, two Marion County sheriff's deputies and a person being interviewed. None of the four is suspected of making the tape.

He said the AG's investigator does not remember who made the racial comments and that it was a matter for local officials to pursue.

"One of (the deputies) will have to own up to whether they made the statement or not," Martin said. "I think it's an issue for the sheriff's department to deal with."

Warren said the official explanation as to who was at the meeting has changed over time.

Warren says he was told by Martin in August that a DOC employee was present at the meeting. That DOC employee named by Martin no longer works for the agency, and Warren said

Continued on Page 7C

Racist
From Page 2C

he's since received conflicting information.

"The first time we met they should have known who was there. It should have been consistent from day one," Warren said. "The only thing one can assume is that they have the facts and they're trying to cover them up."

DOC Commissioner Robert Johnson, in a telephone interview, said only that a DOC official did not make the statements. He did not confirm or deny that a DOC official was present.

"My concern is whether or not any inappropriate utterances or conversations were engaged in by DOC investigators," Johnson said. "At this point, I'm satisfied that that isn't the case."

Johnson stressed that he considers the tape a side show to the main issue of whether the Marion-Walthall facility is being run properly, and said the firings of former warden Fancher and assistant warden James Harvey were appropriate.

Marion County Sheriff Richard Stringer fired Fancher and Harvey in October, citing "the best interests of the facility." Britton Mosley Sr., the former assistant chief of security, was also fired.

Fancher claims he was fired as political payback because he testified before state legislators earlier this year that the DOC was inflating prisoner costs. Harvey and Mosley believe they were fired because they're black.

Sheriff Stringer did not return numerous calls seeking comment.

Johnson said preliminary results from the investigation into the facility "pointed to some irregularities in the operation of the prison," but would not elaborate.

Martin said he expects a case to be presented to the next Marion County grand jury. He wouldn't comment on specifics of potential charges.

The former warden and assistant warden have indicated they likely will file lawsuits over their firings and possibly the tape.

Mosley already has filed a lawsuit in federal court alleging he was fired based on his race.

MISSISSIPPI DEPARTMENT OF CORRECTIONS POLICY NUMBER 03.01			
GENERAL STANDARDS OF PROFESSIONAL CONDUCT	ACA STANDARDS 3-4067		
EFFECTIVE DATE 10-01-97	INITIAL DATE 12-01-82	PAGE	2 OF 2

1 No employee shall accept from or provide to any offender, offender's
2 family, agent, or other representative any gifts or favors.

3 Any employee who becomes aware of any offender with which he has had
4 any previous or existing relationship, whether a kinship
5 relationship (by blood or marriage, adoption, common law) or not;
6 the employee shall immediately report this in writing to his
7 Supervisor/Department Head AND the Superintendent/Community
8 Services Director. The Superintendent/Community Services Director
9 shall immediately report this information in writing to the
10 respective Deputy Commissioners who in turn shall report this
11 information to the Commissioner.

12 No employee shall establish close friendships or fraternize with
13 offenders. The development of any relationship with an offender
14 shall be reported immediately. This reporting shall follow the
15 chain of command listed above.

16 These reports shall include but not be limited to the following:

17 Employee name, social security number, and pin number
18 Employee current work assignment at the time of the report
19 Name of offender, offender number if known, and RELATIONSHIP

20 Employees shall report any unethical, corrupt, or criminal behaviors
21 (if such employees have knowledge that such behaviors are occurring
22 within the department) in such a manner as to ensure that
23 appropriate corrective action is taken.

24 REPORTS REQUIRED:

25 As required by this policy and through the chain of command.

ENFORCEMENT AUTHORITY		
All SOP's and/or other directive documents related to the implementation and enforcement of this policy shall bear the signature of and be issued under the authority of the Commissioner and the Director of Personnel.		
Reviewed and Approved for Issuance	General Counsel	9-3-97 Date
	Commissioner	9-4-97 Date

Fabricating Evidence II

§ 97-1-7

§ 97-1-7. Attempt to commit offense; punishment.

Every person who shall design and endeavor to commit an offense, and shall do any overt act toward the commission thereof, but shall fail therein, or shall be prevented from committing the same, on conviction thereof, shall, where no provision is made by law for the punishment of such offense, be punished as follows: If the offense attempted to be committed be capital, such offense shall be punished by imprisonment in the penitentiary not exceeding ten years; if the offense attempted be punishable by imprisonment in the penitentiary, or by fine and imprisonment in the county jail, then the attempt to commit such offense shall be punished for a period or for an amount not greater than is prescribed for the actual commission of the offense so attempted.

SOURCES: Codes, Hutchinson's 1848, ch. 64, art. 12, Title 8 (3); 1857, ch. 64, art. 20; 1871, § 2809; 1880, § 2713; 1892, § 973; 1906, § 1049; Hemingway's 1917, § 777; 1930, § 793; 1942, § 2017.

Britton Mosley, Sr. & John Fancher

STATE OF MISSISSIPPI
OFFICE OF THE ATTORNEY GENERAL

MIKE MOORE
ATTORNEY GENERAL

PUBLIC INTEGRITY
DIVISION

June 13, 2003

Mr. L.A. Warren
1072 West Lynch Street, Suite 10
Jackson, MS. 39203

Dear Mr. Warren:

Attorney General Moore received your letter dated June 9, 2003, and asked me to respond. You stated that you have not received a response from us concerning an investigation of Marion County Sheriff Richard Stringer and Chief Deputy Rocky Williamson. We have already provided you with such a response. I have enclosed my letter dated April 3, 2002 in which we responded to the allegations against Stringer and Williamson. In addition, as you will recall, we provided you with a copy of our investigative file from the Correctional Facility investigation.

As to the situation involving Mary McKenzie, the conduct does not constitute a violation of M.C.A. §97-3-104 (Rev. 2000). Ms. McKenzie is not employed in one of the positions listed in that statute. I have enclosed a copy of the statute for your review. Thus, she could not be charged with a violation of such statute. Furthermore, I am not aware of any other criminal statute which would be applicable to the situation.

As we have told you before, this office does not engage in selective prosecution. Our actions are based upon the law and the quantity and quality of evidence to support alleged criminal violations.

We appreciate your interest in this matter.

Respectfully,

Lee Martin
Special Assistant Attorney General

/lm

802 N. STATE STREET • P. O. BOX 2 • JACKSON, MS 39205-0012
TELEPHONE (601) 359-4250 • FAX (601) 359-4254

Fabricating Evidence II

☐ Parchman	☐ CMCF	☐ SMCI	☐ CWC

Marion Walthall Correctional Facility

INCIDENT REPORT — Page 2 of 2 Pages

FILE TITLE: Security Operations   CASE STATUS:

BY: CD James Herbin   WITNESS(ES)   RELATED FILES:

AT M.W.C.F.

DATE 4-21-03

REPORT RE: "Inmate and Facility Employee Involved In A Sexual Act"

At apprex. 1754, Nurse Mary McKenzie walked towards the bathroom hile adjusting her clothing. I CD Herbin noticed a large white substance on her pants that appeared to be semen. That was on the back side of the right leg of her pants. I, CD Herbin brought to Nurse McKenzie's attention that there was a big white stain on her pants leg. Nurse McKenzie then proceeded to go on to the bathroom in a rush. I CD Herbin turned back around seeing the examination room where I noticed that inmate Don Brinner had gotten behind the door that was opened to the examining room and started to fix his clothes. Inmate Don Brinner turned to face me, and began to gather his things and I, CD Herbin escorted inmate Don Brinner to D-zone leaving Nurse McKenzie in the bathroom of the infirmary. I, CD Herbin reported this incident to Sgt. Dwayne Allen and IC Alphonso Lyles.

End of Report

SIGNATURE OF OFFICER: James Herbin   APPROVED NAME TITLE: Sgt. Dwayne Allen   DATE: 4/21/03

Marion Walthall Correctional Facility

☐ Parchman   ☐ CMCF   ☐ SMCI   ☐ CWC

INCIDENT REPORT   Page 1 of 2 Pages

FILE TITLE: Security Operations   CASE STATUS:

BY: CD James Herbin   WITNESS(ES):   RELATED FILES:
AT M.W.C.F.   ()
                                                    ()
DATE 4-21-03   ()
                                                    ()

REPORT RE: "Inmate and Facility Employee Involved In A Sexual Act"

At approx. 1750 on the above date, I, CD James Herbin went to the infirmary to let Nurse Mary McKenzie and inmate Don Brinner know that it was time for the certified count. I, CD Herbin entered the infirmary and noticed that there was no one in the front part of the infirmary. CD Herbin then proceeded to go to the back of the infirmary to the examination area, where I walked upon Nurse McKenzie and inmate Don Brinner ingaging in a sexual act. I, CD Herbin noticed that Nurse Mae McKenzie was laying across the edge of the examining table with her pants slightly lowered around her ~~thighs~~ upper thigh area, and inmate Don Brinner's pants were lowered at approx. the area of his upper thighs. When both Nurse McKenzie and inmate Don Brinner realized that I was in the room they were startled, and shocked and began to panic which caused them to act as if they were trying to cover up what they were doing. Inmate Don Brinner fell to the floor pretending to look for an earring. I, CD Herbin asked inmate Don Brinner (4) times to come out of the infirmary for the certified count but inmate Don Brinner made no attempt to come out of the infirmary, but asked to let him gather his things while continuing to sit on the floor. Inmate Don Brinner then grabbed a shirt off the examining table, opened it up, and tried to cover himself up while trying to keep his pants from falling down further.

SIGNATURE OF OFFICER   APPROVED NAME TITLE   DATE
[signature]   Sgt. [signature]   4/21/03

Fabricating Evidence II

NATIONAL ASSOCIATION FOR THE ADVANCEMENT OF COLORED PEOPLE
MISSISSIPPI STATE CONFERENCE

June 09, 2003

EUGENE BRYANT, SR.
President

George Robers
1st Vice President

Curley Clark
2nd Vice President

Melvin Hollins
3rd Vice President

Derrick Johnson
4th Vice President

Kelvin Buck
5th Vice President

Eddie Smith
6th Vice President

Janet Self
Secretary

Dorothy Isaac
Asst. Secretary

James Crowell
Treasurer

James Crear
Asst. Treasurer

Dear Mike,

I am writing this letter in reference to the investigation of the Marion/Walthall Correctional Facility, which your office conducted in 2001. At the conclusion of your initial investigation, the State NAACP filed a formal complaint and requested a full investigation of Marion County Sheriff Richard Stringer and Chief Deputy Rocky Williamson as a result of evidence obtained during our own investigation. We have as of yet to receive a written response from your office as to the findings of this investigation. Because of the considerable time that has lapsed since the filing of the complaint, you can understand our concern.

There also seems to be another disturbing pattern developing in Marion County. During your initial investigation your office indicted and prosecuted a former employee Charles Evans, a black male, for falsifying a travel expense voucher. Well, we have received information that a white female, Mary McKenzie, who was employed as a nurse at the Marion County Facility was caught on April 21, 2003 by a corrections officer having sex with a state inmate in the facility infirmary (SEE ENCLOSED REPORT). We understand the Commissioner of Corrections, Chris Epps, as well as your office have been notified of this violation of state statue 97-3-104. At the time of this letter we know of no charges having been brought against Mrs. McKenzie either by the Marion County Sheriff's office or your office. This type of selective prosecution of persons at the Marion County facility concerns us greatly.

We are asking that you please forward us a written report of the findings or conclusion of your investigation of Sheriff Stringer and Chief Deputy Williamson. We also request that you look into this blatant violation of law concerning the nurse having sex with a state inmate.

Thanking you in advance,

L.A. Warren
MSC Legal Redress Chairman

Cc: Hannibal Kemerer, Region V General Council
Charles White, Region V Director

1072 West Lynch Street • Suite 10 • Jackson, Mississippi 39203 • (601) 353-6906 • 1-800-80NAACP • FAX (601) 353-1565

Britton Mosley, Sr. & John Fancher

STATE OF MISSISSIPPI
OFFICE OF THE ATTORNEY GENERAL

MIKE MOORE
ATTORNEY GENERAL

PUBLIC INTEGRITY
DIVISION

January 18, 2002

Commissioner Robert Johnson
Department of Corrections
723 North President Street
Jackson, MS. 39202

Re: Marion / Walthall County Correctional Facility Investigation

Dear Commissioner:

As you are aware, our offices conducted a joint investigation concerning alleged wrongdoing at the Marion/Walthall County Correctional Facility. The following is a brief summary of the various allegations which were investigated and the findings:

There were allegations that Warden Fancher and Assistance Warden Harvey were using the property of the facility and inmate labor for their personal benefit. Specifically, these allegations included claims that work was performed on boats owned by Fancher and Harvey using materials from the facility and inmates performed the work. While the inmates admit working on the boats, there is some uncertainty as to who provided the materials. We could not prove with any certainty that the facility's materials were used to do the work. There was also a similar allegation concerning a deer stand built for Harvey. Likewise, while the inmates admit doing the work, there is some uncertainty as to who provided the materials.

As a result of our investigation, there will be no criminal charges or ethics violations pursued against either Fancher or Harvey. As you are aware, Fancher and Harvey were terminated from their positions with the correctional facility. My office had no involvement in the decision to terminate them nor were the findings of our investigation turned over to Sheriff Stringer who made the decision to terminate them.

Inmate Willie Brown was cooking and selling plates of food to other inmates in the facility. The private food service employees stated that after taking an order from the correctional facility, Brown would then place his order over the phone for steaks, chicken and pork chops. When the food was delivered a kitchen worker would sign a ticket for the

802 N. STATE STREET • P. O. BOX 2 • JACKSON, MS 39205-0002
TELEPHONE (601) 359-4250 • FAX (601) 359-4254

Fabricating Evidence II

MISSISSIPPI DEPARTMENT OF CORRECTIONS POLICY	DOC. 03-01
GENERAL STANDARDS OF PROFESSIONAL CONDUCT	ACA STANDARDS: 3-3068, 3-3069, 3-4067 & 4-ACRS-3A-07
§ 97-3-97, House Bill 59 (1998)	RESTRICTED
EFFECTIVE DATE: 10-01-02	INITIAL DATE: 12-01-82	PAGE 2 of 3

- Employees will report any unethical, corrupt, or criminal behaviors occurring within the department to their supervisor, Internal Audit Division, or the Director of Personnel.

- No employee will accept from or provide to any offender or their immediate family any item not authorized by the MDOC, nor will any employee accept from or provide to any offender or their immediate family any item in a manner not authorized by MDOC.

- No employee will establish close friendships or fraternize with offenders or their immediate family, agent or other representative.

Any employee who becomes aware of any offender with whom he has had any previous or existing relationship, whether a kinship relationship (by blood or marriage, adoption, common law) or not, the employee will immediately report this in writing to his Supervisor or Department Head and the Superintendent or Community Corrections Director. The Superintendent or Community Corrections Director will immediately report this information in writing to the respective Deputy Commissioners who in turn will report this information to the Commissioner.

House Bill 59, signed by the Governor on March 26, 1998, states - "It will be unlawful for any jailer, guard, employee of the Department of Corrections, sheriff, constable, marshal, or other officer to engage in any sexual penetration as defined in Section 97-3-97, Mississippi Code of 1972, with any offender, with or without the offender's consent, who is incarcerated at any jail or any state, county or private correctional facility. Any person who violates this section will be guilty of a felony and upon conviction will be fined not more than Five Thousand Dollars ($5,000) or imprisoned for a term not to exceed five (5) years, or both."

Employees will not discriminate against any individual because of race, gender, creed, national origin, religious affiliation, age or any other type of prohibited discrimination.

REPORTS REQUIRED:

As required by this policy and through the chain of command.

Ex-guard found in Texas faces jail sex charge

By Mark F. Bonner
mark.bonner@rankinledger.com

A former prison guard accused of having sex with an inmate was brought back to Rankin County last week after allegedly dodging police in San Antonio for more than a year.

A U.S. Marshals Service task force arrested Jennifer Danielle Readus, 22, last month in San Antonio.

"Acting on a tip, we were able to provide U.S. marshals in Texas with an address, which helped develop our investigation," said supervisory Deputy Marshal Richard Griffin.

The indictment alleges Readus, then an officer at the Central Mississippi Correctional Facility in Pearl, had sex in May 2006 with 28-year-old inmate Zachariah Combs.

On Nov. 9, 2006, a warrant was issued for Readus' arrest after she failed to appear in Rankin County Circuit Court to answer the indictment.

Before U.S. marshals took the case last month, the Mississippi Department of Corrections was investigating.

"We got the case on Jan. 18 and picked her up on Jan. 25," he said. Multiple phone calls to the MDOC were not returned Friday.

Griffin was unable to provide details of Readus' arrest. A San Antonio *Express-News* Web site reported Readus had been living on San Antonio's west side, working as a telemarketer. She was arrested at her office without incident.

Her family told a reporter they all moved to the south Texas city after Hurricane Katrina and knew nothing about any formal charges.

But the Lone Star Fugitive Task Force, a division of the U.S. Marshals Service, says the former officer was evading arrest.

"She's a young lady with no criminal history other than this," said Tom Smith, with the task force. "But apparently it bothered her enough that she fled Mississippi and she didn't stay to answer her charges."

Calls to Rankin County Sheriff Ronnie Pennington seeking additional details were unsuccessful.

Readus was released from the Rankin County Jail after posting $20,000 bond.

Rankin County District Attorney Michael Guest said Readus will be back in court Aug. 28.

Fabricating Evidence II

This is a formal complaint against Sheriff Richard Stringer of the Marion County Sheriff's Department.

The allegations are: Sheriff Richard Stringer of the Marion County Sheriff's Department made sworn false statements to cause an investigation against Captain Britton Mosley of the Marion Walthall Correctional Facility.

Facts: In April or May of 2001, Sheriff Richard Stringer contacted the Mississippi Attorney General's Office and made false allegations of criminal misconduct against Captain Britton Mosley which caused an extensive investigation by the Attorney General's Office. This is in violation of state statute 97-7-37.

Britton Mosley, 8

§ 97-7-35

by the State of Mississippi, and any person or persons violating the provisions of this section shall be guilty of the crime of false swearing which is created by this section, a felony, and upon conviction thereof, shall be punished by imprisonment in the county jail for not less than six (6) months nor more than five (5) years in the penitentiary, or a fine of not less than one hundred dollars ($100.00), nor more than one thousand dollars ($1,000.00), or by both such fine and imprisonment.

(2) Corroboration or proof by more than one witness to establish the falsity of testimony or statements under oath is not required in prosecutions under this section. It shall not be necessary to prove, to sustain or charge under this section, that the oath or matter sworn to was material, or, if before an executive, legislative or judicial tribunal committee or commission that the tribunal committee or commission had jurisdiction.

Laws 1960, Ch. 256, §§ 1, 2, eff. from and after passage (approved May 5, 1960).

Historical and Statutory Notes

Derivation:
Code 1942, § 2155.5.

Cross References

Perjury, see § 97-9-59 et seq.
Standard state assessment in addition to all court imposed fines or other penalties for any felony violation, see § 99-19-73.

Library References

Encyclopedias
Key Numbers
C.J.S. Perjury §§ 2 to 3, 5 to 8, 21.
Perjury ⚖1.
WESTLAW Topic No. 297.

Hear say List

§ 97-7-37. Sworn false statements to cause investigation

(1) It shall be unlawful for any person or persons to wilfully make any oral or written sworn false statements or affidavit or attestation or complaint or allegation before any individual or officer authorized to administer oaths, that such person or persons or other persons have been or are about to be deprived of any right or privilege or immunity granted or secured by the United States Constitution and laws, or either, or by the Mississippi Constitution and laws, or either, knowing the same, or any material part thereof to be false, with the intent or purpose to cause or encourage an investigation or which causes or contributes in any way to causing an investigation thereof, or any other action to be taken as a result thereof by any executive or legislative or judicial department, officer or agent, or representative of the United States, including but not limited to any member of the Federal Bureau of Investigation or member or representative or employee of, the Commission on Civil Rights created by an act of the Congress of the United States, or the State Advisory Group or Council, or Committee of the Commission on Civil Rights appointed in or for the State of Mississippi, and any person or persons violating the provisions of this section shall be guilty of the crime of false swearing which is created by this section, a felony, and upon conviction thereof, shall be punished

496

CRIMES AGAINST GOVERNMENT § 97-7-39

by imprisonment in the county jail for not less than six (6) months nor more than five (5) years in the penitentiary, or a fine of not less than one hundred dollars ($100.00), nor more than one thousand dollars ($1,000.00), or by both such fine and imprisonment.

(2) Corroboration or proof by more than one witness to establish the falsity of testimony or statements under oath is not required in prosecutions under this section. It shall not be necessary to prove, to sustain any charge under this section, that the oath or matter sworn to was material, or, if before an executive, legislative or judicial tribunal, committee, or commission that the tribunal, committee, or commission had jurisdiction.

Laws 1960, Ch. 255, §§ 1, 2, eff. from and after passage (approved May 11, 1960).

Historical and Statutory Notes

Derivation:
Code 1942, § 2155.6.

Cross References

Perjury, see § 97-9-59 et seq.
Standard state assessment in addition to all court imposed fines or other penalties for any felony violation, see § 99-19-73.

Library References

Key Numbers
Perjury ⚖=1.
WESTLAW Topic No. 297.

Encyclopedias
C.J.S. Perjury §§ 2 to 3, 5 to 8, 21.

§ 97-7-39. Defacing federal, state, confederate flag

Any person who, in any manner, for exhibition or display, shall place or cause to be placed any word, figure, mark, picture, design, drawing, or any advertisement of any nature, upon any flag, standard, color or ensign of the United States or state flag of the State of Mississippi, or ensign or Confederate flag, or shall expose or cause to be exposed to public view any such flag, standard, color or ensign, upon which shall be attached, appended, affixed or annexed any word, figure, mark, picture, design or drawing, or any advertisement of any nature, or who shall expose to public view, manufacture, sell, expose for sale, give away or have in possession for sale or to give away, or for use for any purpose, any article or substance, being an article of merchandise, or a receptacle of merchandise, or article or things for carrying or transporting merchandise upon which, shall have been printed, painted, attached or otherwise placed, a representation of any such flag, standard, color or ensign, to advertise, call attention to, decorate, mark or distinguish the article or substance, on which so placed, or who shall publicly mutilate, deface, defile or defy, trample upon or cast contempt, either by word or act, upon any such flag, standard, color or ensign, with the intent to desecrate or dishonor such, shall be guilty of a misdemeanor and upon conviction shall be punished by a fine of not more than one thousand dollars ($1,000.00), or by imprisonment for not more than thirty (30) days, or both, in the discretion of the court; shall be deemed guilty of a misdemeanor and shall be punished by a fine not exceeding

CHAPTER 5

Termination

John "Jimmy" Fancher

On October 17, 2001, while the state's investigation was ongoing, Warden John "Jimmy" Fancher and Assistant Warden James Harvey were terminated from their duties at Marion/Walthall Correctional Facility. Sheriff Richard "Rip" Stringer issued a press release stating the decision to relieve Jimmy Fancher and James Harvey was based on administrative problems within the facility. However, Jimmy Fancher's retorted that the termination was politically motivated and false allegations for termination. A letter from the state Attorney General's Office, dated January 16, 2002, stated that as a result of their investigation, there would be no criminal charges or violations pursued against either Fancher or Harvey.

Fabricating Evidence II

A letter dated July 15, 2002 from the State Auditor's office stated, "On 5/14/2001, the Office of the Auditor received a complaint/referral against Jimmy Fancher, Warden, alleging the following: "misuse of public funds." After a thorough investigation of the complaint with legal advice from the OSA staff attorney and the Office of the Attorney General, it was determined that the allegation against Jimmy Fancher could not be substantiated." The letter continues that the case involving Fancher was closed on July 15, 2002. Marion County Sheriff Richard "Rip" Stringer released a letter, in which Stringer cited Fancher's firing was in "the best interest" of the facility. However, the evidence shows collusion between the Mississippi Department of Corrections Deputy Commissioner Chris Epps and Sheriff Stringer. Fancher stated his firing was political payback, stemming from his testimony earlier in the year before House and Senate Corrections Committees that the Department of Corrections was inflating inmates cost numbers. Fancher said county regional prisons are more efficient than state-run facilities. Fancher alleges the Sheriff "got in bed with the Mississippi Department of Corrections' Epps" because he had investigated the Sheriff's cousin and Sheriff Deputy for ethics violations. Sheriff Stringer said the allegations were made by staff and citizens of Marion County.

However, Fancher never saw any of the allegations or reports. Jimmy Fancher gained notoriety within Marion County, and the citizens of Marion County wanted him to run for Sheriff in the upcoming election.

Deputy Commissioner Chris Epps stated the Department of Corrections was "working in conjunction with the Attorney General's Office in an investigation of the Marion/Walthall Corrections Facility." Epps said he "didn't know who or what is being investigated," but how could that be true?

"The Mississippi Department of Corrections," Epps said, "must prove the hiring of wardens, but it does not have to approve their firing."

Jimmy Fancher filed a lawsuit in Chancery Court in Hinds County, Mississippi. The suit sought a mandatory injunction, ordering the immediate reinstatement of Fancher's employment, with back pay. The suit also sought preliminary injunction to keep the defendants from making public statements about unfounded criminal activities allegedly committed by Fancher. Chancellor Stuart Robinson's conclusion was, "This court has heard testimony and finds that political motivations likely played a significant role in the discharge of Fancher. However, this court is without the authority to address this issue as there is no valid contract in this case." Fancher had worked under a Marion County Board of Supervisors approved contract for over two years. However, Judge Stuart Robinson "finds that Defendant is entitled to judgement as a matter of law as the agreement was not a legal and properly recorded action of the Marion County Board of Supervisors and thereby not a valid contract. Therefore, this court grants Defendant's motion for Summary Judgement in accordance with Mississippi Rule of Civil Procedure 56."

Jimmy Fancher attempted to restore his correctional career. Several correctional facilities offered him employment, but were derailed and blocked by Department of Corrections' Commissioner Chris Epps. This is how Fancher's career in corrections ended by illegitimate political connections and retaliation.

Britton Mosley, Sr.'s Termination

In mid-October 2001, shortly after Sheriff Richard "Rip" Stringer fired Jimmy Fancher from his job as Warden at the Marion/Walthall Corrections Facility, Britton Mosley, Sr., was on administrative leave to use up some of the many comp time hours after working long hours during the American Correctional Association audit.

While driving on U.S. Highway 84 in Wayne County, Mississippi, Mosley's van developed engine problems. He increased his speed in order to get to the next exit. Mississippi State Trooper Daryl Woodson pulled Mosley over on a speeding violation. After explaining his problem to Trooper Woodson, Mosley told him he was a law enforcement officer also. Trooper Woodson called the Marion County Sheriff's Department and talked with Captain Doug Barnes, who told Trooper Woodson to take Mosley's badge and arrest him for impersonating a law enforcement officer. Trooper Woodson wanted to know what in the hell was going on. After Mosley explained his side of the story to Trooper Woodson, he kept Mosley's badge and escorted him to the next exit. He refused to arrest Mosley.

On October 31, 2001, Mosley received a letter from Sheriff Richard "Rip" Stringer, announcing his termination for unexcused absences. However, Mosley had approval and proof that he was on administrative leave approved by Jimmy Fancher, when he was still Warden.

Mosley believes this act by Sheriff Stringer was an act of retaliation because of Mosley's January 5, 2001 EEOC charge of discrimination against Marion County Sheriff's Department. On September 6, 2001, Mosley was interviewed by Roger Cribb, Criminal Investigator for the State Attorney General's Office. Cribb informed Mosley of criminal allegations made against him by Sheriff Stringer. After the Attorney General's investigation was completed, the allegations were proved false. These types of false allegations by law enforcement personnel led to wrongful conviction of too many African Americans in Mississippi. Thus, how Mississippi became second in mass incarceration in America, by incarcerating mainly African Americans.

Alleged 'political, racial' firings invite legal battle in Marion County

JACKSON, Miss. (AP) — A battle over control of the Marion-Walthall Correctional Facility is brewing after the sheriff fired the warden and assistant warden — a move the two men say was based on politics and race.

Warden Jimmy Fancher and Assistant Warden James Harvey were fired by Marion County Sheriff Richard "Rip" Stringer last month in a letter, in which Stringer cited "the best interests" of the facility.

Fancher says his firing is political payback stemming from his testimony earlier this year before House and Senate corrections committees that the Department of Corrections was inflating prisoner cost numbers.

Fancher has said that county regional prisons are more efficient than state-run facilities.

The former warden alleges the sheriff got in bed with the DOC because Fancher had investigated the sheriff's cousin for ethics breaches.

"Stringer said he had allegations made by the toward the staff and citizens of the county, but to this day I have not seen any allegations or reports," Fancher said.

Fancher's contract with the county says that the warden may be dismissed for "reasonable cause."

Repeated attempts to contact Sheriff Stringer were unsuccessful.

The DOC is working in conjunction with the Attorney General's office in an investigation of the Marion-Walthall facility, said Chris Epps, the DOC deputy commissioner of institutions. Epps said he didn't know who or what is being investigated.

The DOC, Epps said, must approve the hiring of wardens, but it does not have to approve their firing.

Harvey, who is black, says he was fired because of his race.

"I was a black man who focused strictly on doing my job and following procedure," Harvey said. "The Marion County sheriff's department is not a procedure-oriented organization. They want to continue to do things in the good ol' boy mentality."

Members of the state NAACP are to meet with Attorney General Mike Moore Tuesday concerning Harvey's dismissal, L.A. Warren of the NAACP said.

Stringer replaced Fancher with interim warden Joe Mingo, a black man. Harvey was replaced by Johnnie Glover, the sheriff's cousin by marriage.

Joseph M. Shepard, the attorney for the Marion County Supervisors — a party to Fancher's contract with the county — says a contract between the Marion County facility and the DOC appears to conflict with the county contract.

"The (state) inmate housing agreement provides that the warden serves at the will and the pleasure of the sheriff," Shepard said. "And the sheriff could summarily dismiss the warden without consulting with the board of supervisors."

Lawsuit seeks to reinstate Fancher as warden

Court date set for Feb. 11

A court date has been set for Feb. 11 to hear a request that Jimmy Fancher be returned immediately to his position as warden at the Marion/Walthall Correctional Facility, from which he was fired last year.

The request for injunctive relief is included in a suit filed by Fancher against Sheriff Richard "Rip" Stringer, Marion County and the Mississippi Department of Corrections.

The suit, filed Jan. 15 in Chancery Court in Hinds County, states, in part:

"Fancher seeks a mandatory injunction ordering that Fancher's employment shall be reinstated immediately with back pay, attorney fees and interest and any other damages applicable in the premises. Fancher seeks a preliminary injunction enjoining the defendants from making public statements about unfounded criminal activities allegedly committed by Fancher."

The suit, which gives only one side of a legal argument, claims that sometime around April 2001, Stringer instigated an investigation that was conducted by representatives of the state Attorney

See Lawsuit, Page 2

Lawsuit... From Page 1

General's office, Department of Corrections and local sheriff's department. In October, Fancher was fired.

The suit continues that "Stringer was without authority to terminate Fancher's employment without approval of the board. Defendant Stringer was without justification to terminate Fancher's employment whether with or without the board's approval.

None of the defendants had justification to terminate Fancher's employment."

Fancher's attorney, John Reeves, said defendants in the suit were served Wednesday. Marion County Chancery Clerk Cass Barnes and a secretary with the sheriff's department said Thursday morning, however, that they had not yet seen the suit.

Reeves said the next step in the suit will be the Feb. 11 court date unless defendants in the suit take some action prior to that time.

IN THE CHANCERY COURT OF THE FIRST JUDICIAL DISTRICT
OF HINDS COUNTY, MISSISSIPPI

JIMMY FANCHER   PLAINTIFF

VS.   CIVIL ACTION NO. G-2002-63 R/1

MARION COUNTY, MISSISSIPPI, BY AND
THROUGH ITS BOARD OF SUPERVISORS;
RICHARD STRINGER, MARION COUNTY
SHERIFF; and MISSISSIPPI DEPARTMENT
OF CORRECTIONS   DEFENDANTS

FILED SEP 04 2002
L. GLYNN PEPPER, CHANCERY CLERK

OPINION AND ORDER OF THE COURT

BEFORE THIS COURT is Defendants' Motion for Summary Judgment. This Court has considered all pleadings, depositions, answers to interrogatories, and admissions on file, together with those affidavits provided, and finds that Defendant's Motion for Summary Judgment is well taken and should be granted.

Plaintiff's complaint was stated in two counts, one for breach of contract and the second seeking injunctive relief. The claim for injunctive relief has been denied by prior order of this Court entered April 9, 2002. Therefore, the only claims remaining before this Court are the allegations of breach of contract.

Plaintiff was employed, commencing in November, 1998, by Marion County to serve as warden of the Marion Walthall Correctional Facility. In February 2000, the Plaintiff (hereinafter "Fancher"), Defendant Richard Stringer, Marion County Sheriff (hereinafter "Sheriff") and Calvin Newsom, President of the Marion County Board of Supervisors signed a document entitled

1

"Employment Agreement" specifying salary, duration and termination. This agreement is the basis for Plaintiff's breach of contract claim.

In April 2001, Sheriff Stringer instigated an investigation into the Marion Walthall Correctional Facility and Fancher. The investigation was conducted by representatives of the Mississippi Attorney General's office, Mississippi Department of Corrections and Marion County Sheriff's Department. On October 17, 2001, Fancher was asked to resign from his position as Warden due to the investigation. Fancher refused, and on October 22, 2001, Sheriff Stringer confirmed that Fancher was fired, effective October 31, 2001. Fancher claims that his discharge was politically motivated and wholly unwarranted; therefore, he seeks damage for breach of contract. This Court has heard testimony and finds that political motivations likely played a significant role in the discharge of Fancher; however, this Court is without the authority to address this issue as there is no valid contract in this case.

DISCUSSION

Mississippi Rule of Civil Procedure 56 (c) states that a Motion for Summary Judgment shall be granted if "there is no genuine issue as to any material fact and . the moving party is entitled to a judgment as a matter of law." Miss. R. Civ. P. 56 (c) (1998). Our Mississippi Supreme Court has further opined that where an action presents only a legal question, summary judgment is appropriate. *Smith v. First Federal Savings & Loan Association of Grenada*, 460 So. 2d 786 (Miss. 1984). This Court has entertained testimony and argument in the Preliminary Injunction Hearing, as well as argument during the summary judgment motion hearing, and is convinced that there is no genuine issue as to any material fact

Summary Judgment is appropriate in this instance as only a legal question remains. The only issue to be determined by the Court is whether an enforceable contract existed between Plaintiff and Defendants. This Court finds that no enforceable contract existed. It is undisputed that some of the parties signed a piece of paper which was styled "Employment Agreement." However, it is basic Mississippi law that:

> An officer shall not enter into any contract on behalf of the state, or of any county, city, town or village thereof, without being specially authorized thereto by law or by an order of the board of supervisors or municipal authorities.

Mississippi Code Annotated § 25-1-43. In the case at hand, the issue is whether the Sheriff and the President of the Board of Supervisors were "specially authorized" to enter into the alleged contract. It is a well established tenet of Mississippi law that "[a] Board of Supervisors can act only as a body, and its act must be evidenced by an entry on its minutes. The minutes of the board of supervisors are the sole and exclusive evidence of what the board did." *Nichols v. Patterson*, 678 So. 2d 673, 677 (Miss 1996) (quoting *Smith v. Board of Supervisors of Tallahatchie County*, 86 So. 707, 709 (Miss 1921)). In the instant case, all parties agree that the purported employment agreement was not spread on the minutes of the Board of Supervisors.

Plaintiff relies on *Community Extended Care Center, Inc. v Board of Supervisors for Humphreys County, Mississippi and Humphreys County, Mississippi*, 756 So. 2d 798 (Miss 1999) (rehearing denied 1999) for the proposition that this contract may be enforced through equitable estoppel. However, Plaintiff's reliance is misplaced. This Court has closely read this opinion and agrees with Plaintiff that the Mississippi Supreme Court found the county to be equitably estopped from arguing that the lease was invalid for failure to spread across the minute book. However, that case is clearly distinguishable from this case and previous case law. Our Mississippi Supreme Court has consistently held that "the doctrine of equitable estoppel cannot be applied against the state or its counties where the acts of their officers were unauthorized." *Rawls Springs Utility District v. Novak*, 765 So. 2d 1288, 1292 (Miss. 2000) (citing *Oktibbeha County Board of Education v. Town of Sturgis*, 531 So. 2d 585, 589 (Miss. 1988)). The decision in *CECC* did not change this line of cases; rather it reiterated this precedent. In *CECC*, the Board passed a resolution that was duly and lawfully spread upon its minutes. This resolution showed that the supervisors unanimously approved the lease with CECC and authorized the Board president to sign the lease on behalf of the Board. So, although the lease was not spread on the minutes, the resolution authorizing the Board president to sign the lease was spread on the minutes. Therefore, the acts of the Board president were not unauthorized and equitable estoppel applied.

In the case *sub judice*, there is no employment agreement spread on the minutes of the board. Likewise, there is no resolution or other action authorizing the Board president to sign such agreement spread on the minutes of the board. Clearly, this case is distinguishable on all counts from that of *Community Extended Care Center, Inc. v Board of Supervisors for Humphreys County, Mississippi and Humphreys County, Mississippi*, 756 So. 2d 798 (Miss. 1999) (rehearing denied 1999).

CONCLUSION

After hearing, this Court concludes that there exists no genuine issue of material facts as to this cause of action. Further, this Court finds that Defendants are entitled to judgment as a matter of law, as the agreement was not a legal and properly recorded action of the Marion

County Board of Supervisors and is thereby not a valid contract. Therefore, this Court grants Defendant's Motion for Summary Judgment in accordance with Mississippi Rule of Civil Procedure 56.

SO ORDERED, ADJUDGED, AND DECREED THIS the 4TH day of September, 2002.

CHANCELLOR STUART ROBINSON

Fabricating Evidence II

RICHARD "Rip" STRINGER, Sheriff
Marion County
500 Courthouse Square, Suite 1
COLUMBIA, MS 39429
601-736-5051

October 30, 2001

Mr. Britton Mosley
P. O. Box 390
700 Butler Twyner Road
State Line, MS 39362

Dear Mr. Mosley:

As you well know, you have been absent from work since October 17, and you have provided me with no explanation whatsoever.

Your conduct leaves me with no choice but to terminate your employment with the Marion-Walthall Correctional Facility, effective October 17, 2001. All equipment issued to you is to be returned to the facility on or before November 10, 2001.

Sincerely,

Richard "Rip" Stringer
Sheriff, Marion County, Mississippi

RWS:ph

e7/1

J. Darryl Madison

Received Badge From Britton Mosley Per Request of Capt Barnes, Because Subject Has Been Terminated.

Fabricating Evidence II

Third employee fired from prison

Investigations continues at correctional facility

By Dana Gower
Staff Writer

Following last month's firing of the warden and assistant warden at the Marion/Walthall Correctional Facility, a third employee said he found out from a Mississippi Highway Patrol trooper he had been fired, and another employee has been notified her position has been cut back to part time.

Britton "Britt" Mosley Sr., the former assistant chief of security at the correctional facility, said this week he learned he had been fired when he was pulled over during a traffic stop. Mosley said he had been on administrative leave since about Oct. 12 while a series of investigations were underway at the prison facility.

On Oct. 30, Mosley said, he was pulled over for allegedly speeding, which he denies. Mosley said that, after he told the trooper he was employed at the correctional facility, the trooper called in that information and was informed Mosley no longer worked there. Mosley said that on Thursday, Oct. 31, he received a letter telling him of his termination.

Since, to his knowledge, the investigations are still underway at the prison, Mosley said he doesn't understand why he was fired while he was already on leave.

Gennett Daniels, food service director at the facility, said she was notified Friday that her position was being reduced to part

See Prison, Page 2A

Britton Mosley, Sr. & John Fancher

February 12, 2002

TO WHOM IT MAY CONCERN:

This letter is to verify that Captain Britton Mosley, Sr. requested and received administrative leave for personal reasons. This administrative leave began on October 15, 2001, and extended through November 7, 2001.

[signature]
James Harvey, Former Deputy Warden
Marion Walthall Correctional Facility

[signature]
Jimmy Fancher, Former Warden
Marion Walthall Correctional Facility

Judge overturns benefits award to fired correctional employee

By Dana Gower
Staff Writer

A ruling awarding unemployment benefits to one of the officials fired from the Marion/Walthall Correctional Facility has been overturned by Circuit Judge R.I. Prichard.

Prichard's law clerk said this week that the order and final judgment calls for a new hearing to be held on whether Britton "Britt" Mosley Sr., formerly the assistant chief of security at the facility, is entitled to unemployment benefits. Mosley's attorney could not be reached for comment concerning the ruling.

Mosley, who was fired last October, the same month that the facility's warden and assistant warden were relieved of their positions by Marion County Sheriff Richard "Rip" Stringer, said at the time of his dismissal that he learned he had been fired when he was pulled over during a traffic stop.

On Oct. 30, 2001, Mosley said, he was pulled over for allegedly speeding. After he told the trooper he was employed at the correctional facility, the trooper called in that information and was told Mosley no longer worked there.

An order filed with the Marion County Circuit Clerk's office on June 24 in the suit filed by Stringer and the Marion County Sheriff's Department against Mosley and the Mississippi Employment Security Commission states, "Mosley filed for unemployment benefits, effective date Nov. 2, 2001, after being terminated from his employment at the Marion Walthall Correctional Facility for failing to come to work for three days without notice to his employer..Mosley claimed he thought he was on administrative leave due to pending investigations of the correctional facility. The claims examiner denied benefits on Nov. 20, 2001 finding that Mosley's unexcused absences constituted misconduct...Mosley appealed the claims examiner's decision to the appeals referee and a telephonic hearing was scheduled for Dec. 13, 2001. This is where the sheriff's department's problems began."

According to the order, Stringer claimed the sheriff's department never received notification of the hearing.

"Since the sheriff's department did not 'attend' the hearing, and since they, as the employer, had the burden of showing Mosley was terminated for misconduct, the appeals referee found that the sheriff's department had not met their burden of proof and reversed the decision of the claims referee," the order states. "More problems ensued when the sheriff's department did not timely appeal the decision of the appeals referee within the allotted time. The board of review stated since the sheriff's department had not..filed their appeal within 14 days of the decision dated Dec. 14, 2001 that the decision of the appeals referee had become final and dismissed the appeal. It is from this decision of the board of review that the instant appeal has been taken."

The order continues that, "The record in this case is completely bereft of any evidence whatsoever upon which the appeals referee based his decision other than the sheriff's department's failure to 'attend' for failure of the appeals referee to call them...The court has absolutely no hesitation in reversing MESC on this ground...There is no record of when the sheriff's department received their notification of the appeals referee's decision reversing the claims examiner. The sheriff's department mailed their notice of appeal on Dec. 31, 2001 and it was received by MESC on Jan. 2, 2002. On Jan. 10, 2002, the board of review, who had the exact same information before it that this court has now, stubbornly clung to the tardiness of the sheriff's department's appeal in upholding the appeals referee's decision as the final decision."

CHAPTER 6

Equal Employment Opportunity Commission's Charge of Discrimination

In January 2001, former Captain Britton Mosley, Sr., filed an Equal Employment Opportunity Commission claim of discrimination against the Marion County Sheriff's Department. After being promoted to Assistant Chief of Security in February 2000, Mosley was subjected to verbal harassment, physical threats, and attempted conspiracy to plant illegal drugs on his possession. Chief of Security Johnny Glover circulated false rumors to staff members about him. Glover finished the in-house training academy, and Mosley was one of the instructors. Chief of Security Glover didn't have any correctional experience. However, he was Mosley's boss. Sheriff Richard "Rip" Stringer promoted Mosley to be Glover's assistant; Mosley had to do his job. Glover's dislike for Mosley was well known throughout the

Sheriff's Department, where Glover had the rank of Major. He was also the sheriff's cousin by marriage.

There was an ongoing situation of racism and injustice between Sheriff Stringer, Major Glover, and Mosley. Compelling evidence will show the graphic sexual comments and racial slurs made by staff members of the Marion County Sheriff's Department. The staff members also made false criminal allegations against Mosley. Sheriff Stringer refused to take any disciplinary action against these employees because Sheriff Stringer, himself, was implicated in the complaints. Mosley filed two complaints with the Equal Employment Opportunity Commission (Charge Numbers 131-A1-0457 and 131-A2-00546) of retaliation.

The Equal Employment Opportunity Commission determined the evidence obtained in their investigation established reasonable cause to believe the charging party was discriminated against. The Marion County Sheriff's Department was in validation of Title VII of the Civil Rights Act of 1964, as amended. The Equal Employment Opportunity Commission issued two favorable determinations. In August 2001, the US Department of Justice issued a notice of Right to Sue against the Marion County Sherriff's Department.

Britton Mosley, Sr. & John Fancher

he Columbian-Progress

EEOC favors worker fired from prison

Despite a determination by the U.S. Equal Employment Opportunity Commission favoring the claim of a former Marion-Walthall Correctional Facility employee that his firing was retaliatory, an attorney representing the Marion County Sheriff's Department said the claim is without merit.

Britt Mosley Sr. was notified in October of 2001 that he had been terminated from his position as assistant chief of security at the correctional facility. Mosley said he was on administrative leave at the time.

A letter dated March 24 from the EEOC states Mosley claimed he was retaliated against because he filed a charge of discrimination against the sheriff's department on Jan. 5, 2001.

"I have determined that the evidence obtained in the investigation establishes reasonable cause to believe that (Mosley) was discriminated against...in that (he) was discharged on Oct. 30, 2001, while he was on a leave of absence approved by the Deputy Warden for the period Oct. 17, 2001, through November 2001," the letter states.

"The granting of this leave was as per the policies in effect at this time. The sheriff was not required to approve leave for employees in the correctional facility at that time. The policies which required him to approve leave became effective on Nov. 5, 2001. (Mosley) was already on leave under the old policies at that time."

Vicksburg attorney Ken Rector, who is representing the sheriff's office in cases arising from the firing of a number of employees at the correctional facility, said, however, that the EEOC's determination carries no legal weight.

"I don't expect there to be any change in our position," he said, noting that Mosley "was fired for not coming to work by (current warden) Joe Mingo, who is black. It's hard to make a racial discrimination complaint against another black man."

The letter from the EEOC points out, however, that "A white male was granted a verbal leave of absence in January, 2000. There is no evidence that there were any written records on this and no evidence that he was discharged."

Rector also questioned Mosley's contention that he was fired for filing a discrimination charge, citing the amount of time that passed between the time the complaint was filed in January and the time Mosley was fired at the end of October.

"If causation is there, it's usually a fairly short time period," he said.

If Mosley chooses to move ahead with his complaint, Rector said, the only option is to file suit in federal court.

Mosley said this week he intends either to file a new lawsuit, or to amend an existing one that claims he was subjected to a hostile work environment. Rector said a motion for summary judgment in that case is pending, and that he hopes to have a ruling on the motion within 60 days.

Mosley said his firing has had a "profound effect" on him.

"Personally, I feel a disservice was done to me there," he said. "It's caused tremendous hardships for me and my family."

Fabricating Evidence II

SERVING THE CITIZENS OF MARION COUNTY SINCE 1882

The Columbian-Progress

Saturday, August 2, 2003
COLUMBIA, MISSISSIPPI

Trial dates set for prison lawsuits

Trial dates have been set to hear lawsuits filed by two former employees of the Marion-Walthall Correctional Facility, who filed the federal lawsuits following their termination from the facility in October, 2001.

A trial in Southern District Court has been set for Britt Mosley Sr., assistant chief of security at the correctional facility at the time of his termination, on Feb. 4, 2004.

A trial has been set in the same court district for James Harvey Jr., who was deputy warden at the time of his firing, beginning April 26, 2004.

Mosley has claimed his firing was retaliatory because he had filed a charge of discrimination against the Marion County Sheriff's office earlier that year.

"I want the evidence to show the injustice I received at the hands of (Sheriff Richard) 'Rip' Stringer," Mosley said this week. "I think the evidence will speak for itself."

An attorney who is representing the sheriff's department in the cases said earlier that Mosley "was fired for not coming to work...," but a letter from the U.S. Equal Employment Opportunity Commission states an investigation by that agency showed "reasonable cause to believe...(Mosley) was discharged on Oct. 30, 2001, while he was on a leave of absence approved by the Deputy Warden for the period Oct. 17, 2001, through November 2001."

Stringer announced on Oct. 17, 2001 that Harvey and former Warden Jimmy Fancher had been relieved of their duties. A press release issued that day said the action was "based on administrative problems inside the facility," but both Harvey and Fancher disputed that allegation. Harvey said at the time he believed the action was retaliatory and, in his case, racial.

A month before the firings, representatives of the Marion County branch of the NAACP and the Marion County Civic Club had met with the Marion County Board of Supervisors to discuss complaints of alleged racial discrimination at the facility.

Harvey said this week he is looking forward to his case finally going to trial.

"I wish my court date were sooner," he said, adding, "I look forward to going to trial and letting the evidence show the real reason Sheriff Stringer fired me."

121

BRITTON MOSLEY
STATELINE, MS

September 26, 2002

Ms. Barbara Doan
Enforcement Investigator
Jackson Area Office
Equal Employment Opportunity Commission
100 West Capitol Street
Jackson, MS 39201

Dear Ms. Doan:

In September of this year I received information that a possible key component of my case would be the ability to show that the Respondent Respondent (Marion County Sheriff's Department) had placed other employees on administrative leave pending the outcome of an investigation. As you are aware, I was not given this right to due process. I was terminated while an investigation was ongoing and when the investigation cleared me of all false allegations made against me, I was not offered reinstatement to my job. This fact clearly demonstrates that I was fired for motives which had nothing to do with my being investigated. This investigation was requested by Sheriff Stringer and yet he fired me before it was completed.

I have included two documented examples of employees who were placed on administrative leave pending the outcome of an investigation. Both of these employees were returned to work upon completion of the investigation. One example contains an affidavit from former Warden Jimmy Fancher who placed an employee on leave pending an investigation for shooting an escaped inmate in September of 2000. The second example is an officer who was placed on leave pending an investigation for allowing inmates to escape in September 2002.

Both of these cases are documented examples of proper procedure to follow when an officer or other employee is being investigated. In my situation this was not the case.

Fabricating Evidence II

U.S. EQUAL EMPLOYMENT OPPORTUNITY COMMISSION
Jackson Area Office

Dr. A. H. McCoy Federal Building
100 W. Capitol Street, Suite 207
Jackson, MS 39269
(601) 965-4537
TTY (601) 965-4915
FAX (601) 965-5272

Sheriff Richard Stringer
Marion County Sheriff Department
503 Main Street
Columbia, MS 39429

        Charge No.: 131-2003-00546
        Charging Party: Britton Mosley
        Respondent: Marion County Sheriff Department

Dear Sheriff Stringer:

The Commission has determined that efforts to conciliate this charge as required by Section 706(b) of Title VII of the Civil Rights Act of 1964, as amended, have been unsuccessful. This letter constitutes the notice required by Section 1601.25 of the Commission's Procedural Regulations which provides that the Commission shall notify a Respondent in writing when it determines that further conciliation efforts would be futile or non-productive.

No further efforts to conciliate this case will be made by the Commission. Accordingly, we are at this time forwarding the case to EEOC headquarters for review by the Commission and referral to Department of Justice. Title VII requires that the DOJ bring suit against a government, governmental agency or political subdivision.

                                  Sincerely,

5/30/03
Date

                                  Benjamin Bradley, Area Director

cc: Mr. Kenneth B. Rector
    Wheeless, Shappley, Bailess, & Rector, L.L.P
    P. O. Box 991
    Vicksburg, MS 39181-0991

Britton Mosley, Sr. & John Fancher

February 12, 2002

TO WHOM IT MAY CONCERN:

    This letter is to verify that former Captain Britton Mosley, Sr., while employed by the Marion Walthall Correctional Facility requested and received administrative leave for personal reasons. This administrative leave began on October 15, 2001, and extended through November 7, 2001.

James Harvey, Former Deputy Warden
Marion Walthall Correctional Facility

Jimmy Fancher, Former Warden
Marion Walthall Correctional Facility

Fabricating Evidence II

CHARGE OF DISCRIMINATION

This form is affected by the Privacy Act of 1974; See Privacy Act Statement before completing this form.

AGENCY: ☐ FEPA ☒ EEOC
CHARGE NUMBER: 131-A1-0457

_____ and EEOC
State or local Agency, if any

NAME (Indicate Mr., Ms., Mrs.): Mr. Britton Mosley
HOME TELEPHONE (Include Area Code): (601) 848-7447
STREET ADDRESS / CITY, STATE AND ZIP CODE: P. O. Box 390, State Line, MS 39362
DATE OF BIRTH: 09/30/1948

NAMED IS THE EMPLOYER, LABOR ORGANIZATION, EMPLOYMENT AGENCY APPRENTICESHIP COMMITTEE, STATE OR LOCAL GOVERNMENT AGENCY WHO DISCRIMINATED AGAINST ME (If more than one list below.)

NAME: Marion County Sheriff's Department
NUMBER OF EMPLOYEES, MEMBERS: Cat B (101-200)
TELEPHONE (Include Area Code): (601) 736-3621
STREET ADDRESS / CITY, STATE AND ZIP CODE: 503 South Main Street, Columbia, MS 39429
COUNTY: 091

CAUSE OF DISCRIMINATION BASED ON (Check appropriate box(es)):
☒ RACE ☐ COLOR ☐ SEX ☐ RELIGION ☐ NATIONAL ORIGIN
☐ RETALIATION ☐ AGE ☐ DISABILITY ☐ OTHER (Specify)

DATE DISCRIMINATION TOOK PLACE
EARLIEST: 08/12/2000   LATEST: 12/28/2000
☒ CONTINUING ACTION

THE PARTICULARS ARE (If additional space is needed, attach extra sheet(s)):

I was hired by the above employer in April 2000 and was promoted to assistant chief of security around February 2000. Beginning in February 2000 and continuing until the present, I have been subjected to verbal harassment, physical threats, and attempted conspiracy to plant illegal drugs in my possession.

No reasons have been given for these actions.

I believe I am being harassed and discriminated against because of my race (black) in an attempt to discredit me in my position, in violation of Title VII of the Civil Rights Act of 1964.

[EEOC/JAO JAN 0 5 2001 RECEIVED stamp]

I want this charge filed with both the EEOC and the State or local Agency, if any. I will advise the agencies if I change my address or telephone number and cooperate fully with them in the processing of my charge in accordance with their procedures.

I declare under penalty of perjury that the foregoing is true and correct.

Date: 1/5/01
Charging Party (Signature): Britton Mosley

NOTARY - (When necessary for State and Local Requirements)

I swear or affirm that I have read the above charge and that it is true to the best of my knowledge, information and belief.

SIGNATURE OF COMPLAINANT

SUBSCRIBED AND SWORN TO BEFORE ME THIS DATE
(Month, day and year)

EEOC FORM 5 (Rev. 07/99)

FILE COPY

Britton Mosley, Sr. & John Fancher

U.S. EQUAL EMPLOYMENT OPPORTUNITY COMMISSION
Jackson Area Office

Dr. A. H. McCoy Federal Building
100 W. Capitol Street, Suite 207
Jackson, MS 39269
(601) 965-4537
TTY (601) 965-4915
FAX (601) 965-5272

Charge No. 131 A1 0457

BRITTON MOSLEY
P.O. Box 390
State Line, MS 39362   Charging Party

vs.

MARION COUNTY SHERIFF'S DEPARTMENT
503 South Main Street
Columbia, MS 39429   Respondent

DETERMINATION

On behalf of the Commission, I issue the following determination on the merits of the subject charge. All requirements for coverage are met.

Charging Party alleges that he was subjected to verbal harassment, physical threats, and attempted conspiracy to plant illegal drugs in his possession because of his race (black) in violation of Title VII of the Civil Rights Act of 1964, as amended. Charging Party further alleges that he was retaliated against when Respondent refused to pay him comp pay for the February 15, 2001 pay period.

Respondent denies the allegations of harassment and maintains that no adverse employment actions were taken against Charging Party. Respondent further maintains that Charging Party received all pay due him for the pay period in question.

With respect to Charging Party's harassment allegations, I have determined that the evidence obtained was insufficient to establish violations of the statute.

Fabricating Evidence II

With respect to Charging Party's retaliation allegation, it is undisputed that Charging Party had accumulated comp time. Respondent asserted that comp time is recorded and maintained in the Facility's personnel office however it was unable to locate and produce Charging Party's time sheets. Records revealed that Charging Party was paid his full regular salary for every pay period of his employment except the pay period in question (February 15, 2001).

Based on this analysis, I have determined that Charging Party was retaliated against in violation of Title VII of the Civil Rights Act of 1964, as amended, when he was not given his full salary for the pay period.

This determination does not conclude the processing of this charge. EEOC will begin conciliation efforts to resolve all matters where there is reason to believe that violations have occurred.

You are reminded that Federal law prohibits retaliation against persons who have exercised their right to inquire or complain about matters they believe may violate the law. Discrimination against persons who have cooperated in Commission investigations is also prohibited. These protections apply regardless of the Commission's determination on the merits of the charge.

On Behalf of the Commission:

Date: 6/22/01

Benjamin Bradley, Area Director

Enclosures:

    Proposed Conciliation Agreement.

cc: J. Lawson Hester
    Craig Hester Luke & Dodson
    P.O. Box 12005
    Jackson, MS 39236-2005

Britton Mosley, Sr. & John Fancher

Amendment to charge # 131 A1 0457:

I was off work due to an injury from December 18, 2000 to February 2001. I was released to return to work on February 5, 2001 however I didn't return until February 13 due to family matters, personal illness, and jury duty. It was approved that I would use accumulated comp time. On February 15, 2001 I was paid for only two days of the pay period.

The warden said my pay was docked because I didn't have any comp time left.

I believe my pay was docked in retaliation for filing this charge of discrimination in violation of Title VII of the Civil Rights Act of 1964.

I declare under penalty of perjury that the foregoing is true and correct.

2/23/01
Date

Britton Mosley, Sr.
Charging Party

RECEIVED
FEB 26 2001
EEOC / JAO

Fabricating Evidence II

CHARGE OF DISCRIMINATION

This form is affected by the Privacy Act of 1974; See Privacy Act Statement before completing this form.

AGENCY: ☐ FEPA ☒ EEOC

CHARGE NUMBER: 131-A2-0054(?)

_____ and EEOC
State or local Agency, if any

NAME (Indicate Mr., Ms., Mrs.): Mr. Britton Mosley
HOME TELEPHONE (Include Area Code): (601) 848-7447
STREET ADDRESS: P O Box 390, State Line, MS 39362
DATE OF BIRTH: 09/30/1948

NAMED IS THE EMPLOYER, LABOR ORGANIZATION, EMPLOYMENT AGENCY APPRENTICESHIP COMMITTEE, STATE OR LOCAL GOVERNMENT AGENCY WHO DISCRIMINATED AGAINST ME (If more than one list below.)

NAME: Marion County Sheriff's Department
NUMBER OF EMPLOYEES, MEMBERS: Cat A (15-100)
TELEPHONE (Include Area Code): (601) 736-3621
STREET ADDRESS: 503 South Main Street, Columbia, MS 39429
COUNTY: 091

CAUSE OF DISCRIMINATION BASED ON (Check appropriate box(es)):
☐ RACE ☐ COLOR ☐ SEX ☐ RELIGION ☐ NATIONAL ORIGIN
☒ RETALIATION ☐ AGE ☐ DISABILITY ☐ OTHER (Specify)

DATE DISCRIMINATION TOOK PLACE
EARLIEST: 10/30/2001   LATEST: 10/30/2001
☐ CONTINUING ACTION

THE PARTICULARS ARE (If additional space is needed, attach extra sheet(s)):

On January 5, 2001, I filed a charge of discrimination with Equal Employment Opportunity Commission, Jackson Office, against the Marion County Sheriff's Department (Charge Number 131-A1-0457). On September 6, 2001, I was interviewed by Roger Cribb, criminal investigator for the State Attorney General's Office. Mr. Cribb informed me of criminal allegations made against me by Richard "Rip" Stinger, Sheriff of Marion County, MS. After the Attorney Generals investigation was completed, the allegations were proved to be false.

On October 30, 2001, I received a letter from Sheriff Stringer informing me that I had been terminated while I was on administrative leave pending the outcome of the Attorney General's investigation.

I believe this act by the Marion County Sheriff's Department was in retaliation because of my filing a previous charge against this employer which is in violation of Title VII of the Civil Rights Act of 1964, as amended.

RECEIVED FEB - 2 2002 EEOC / JAO

I want this charge filed with both the EEOC and the State or local Agency, if any. I will advise the agencies if I change my address or telephone number and cooperate fully with them in the processing of my charge in accordance with their procedures.
I declare under penalty of perjury that the foregoing is true and correct.

Date: 1/29/02
Charging Party (Signature): Britton Mosley, Sr.

NOTARY - (When necessary for State and Local Requirements)
I swear or affirm that I have read the above charge and that it is true to the best of my knowledge, information and belief.
SIGNATURE OF COMPLAINANT
SUBSCRIBED AND SWORN TO BEFORE ME THIS DATE (Month, day and year)

EEOC FORM 5 (Rev. 07/99)

FILE COPY

Britton Mosley, Sr. & John Fancher

U.S. EQUAL EMPLOYMENT OPPORTUNITY COMMISSION
Jackson Area Office

Dr. A. H. McCoy Federal Building
100 W. Capitol Street, Suite 207
Jackson, MS 39269
(601) 965-4537
TTY (601) 965-4915
FAX (601) 965-5272

Certified No. Z 204 735 983

EEOC Charge Number: 131-A2-00546

Mr. Britton Mosley
P O Box 390
State Line, MS 39362   Charging Party

Marion County Sheriff's Department
503 South Main Street
Columbia, MS 39429   Respondent

DETERMINATION

Under the authority vested in me by the Commission's Procedural Regulations, I issue the following determination on the merits of the subject charge filed under Title VII of the Civil Rights Act of 1964, as amended.

The Respondent is an employer within the meaning of Title VII and all requirements for coverage have been met.

Charging Party alleges that he was retaliated against in violation of Title VII of the Civil Rights Act of 1964, as amended, by discharging him because he filed a charge of discrimination against Respondent, on January 5, 2001. Charging Party also stated that he was informed during an investigation by the Attorney General's Office, that the sheriff made criminal allegations against him.

I have determined that the evidence obtained in the investigation establishes reasonable cause to believe that Charging Party was discriminated against in violation of Title VII of the Civil Rights Act of 1964, as amended, in that Charging Party was discharged on October 30, 2001, while he was on a leave of absence approved by the Deputy Warden for the period October 17, 2001, through November 2001.

The granting of this leave was as per the policies in effect at this time. The Sheriff was not required to approve leave for employees in the correctional facility at that time. The policies which required him to approve leave became effective on November 5, 2001. Charging Party was already on leave under the old policies at that time.

Fabricating Evidence II

We find that the the Sheriff and managers remaining on duty after the discharge of the individual who approved Charging Party's leave, had information at their disposal which would have enabled them to determine that he was indeed on an approved leave.

A White male was granted a verbal leave of absence in January 2000. There is no evidence that there were any written records on this and no evidence that he was discharged.

We find no evidence, other than his filing a previous charge against the Respondent for the action of discharging Charging Party while he was on an approved leave.

We thus find sufficient evidence to determine that Charging Party was discharged in retaliation for his protected activity of filing a charge of discrimination under Title VII of the Civil Rights Act of 1964, as amended.

We failed to find sufficient evidence to determine that a vendetta by the Sheriff against Charging Party was impetus for the investigation by the Attorney General's office, or that the Sheriff made criminal allegations against him. Charging Party was questioned, as were numerous other employees. He was asked about his leave and also activities he engaged in or observed other employees engaging in. The report by the Attorney General's office did not implicate Charging Party in any wrongdoing or even mention his name. We did not find evidence that he was told that the Sheriff made criminal allegations against him

This determination is final. When the Commission finds that violations have occurred, it attempts to eliminate unlawful practices by informal methods of conciliation. Therefore, I invite the parties to join with the Commission in reaching a just resolution of this matter. Disclosure of information obtained by the Commission during the conciliation process will be made only in accordance with the Commission's Procedural Regulations (29 CFR Part 1601.26).

If the Respondent wishes to accept this invitation to participate in conciliation efforts, it may do so at this time by proposing terms for a conciliation agreement; that proposal should be provided to the Commission representative within 14 days of the date of this determination. The remedies for violations of the statutes we enforce are designed to make the identified victims whole and to provide corrective and preventive relief. These remedies may include, as appropriate, an agreement by the Respondent to not engage in unlawful employment practices, placement of identified victims in positions they would have held but for discriminatory actions, back pay, restoration of lost benefits, injunctive relief, compensatory and/or punitive damages, and notice to employees of the violation and the resolution of the claim.

Should the Respondent have further questions regarding the conciliation process or the conciliation terms it would like to propose, we encourage it to contact the assigned Commission representative. Should there be no response from the Respondent in 14 days, we may conclude that further conciliation efforts would be futile or nonproductive.

On Behalf of the Commission:

Date: 3/24/03

Benjamin Bradley, Area Director

Enclosures: Proposed Conciliation Agreement.

cc: Charging Party's Attorney
Respondent's Attorney

Fabricating Evidence II

U.S. Department of Justice

Civil Rights Division

NOTICE OF RIGHT TO SUE
WITHIN 90 DAYS

CERTIFIED MAIL
0922 2048

Employment Litigation Section
P.O. Box 65968
Washington, DC 20035-5968

Mr. Britton Mosley, Sr.
P.O. Box 390
State Line, MS 39362

August 10, 2001

Re: EEOC Charge Against Marion County Sheriff's Dept.
No. 131A10457

Dear Mr. Mosley, Sr.:

Because you filed the above charge with the Equal Employment Opportunity Commission, and more than 180 days have elapsed since the date the Commission assumed jurisdiction over the charge, and no suit based thereon has been filed by this Department, and because you have specifically requested this Notice, you are hereby notified that you have the right to institute a civil action under Title VII of the Civil Rights Act of 1964, as amended, 42 U.S.C. 2000e, et seq., against the above-named respondent.

If you choose to commence a civil action, such suit must be filed in the appropriate Court within 90 days of your receipt of this Notice. If you cannot afford or are unable to retain an attorney to represent you, the Court may, at its discretion, assist you in obtaining an attorney. If you plan to ask the Court to help you find an attorney, you must make this request of the Court in the form and manner it requires. Your request to the Court should be made well before the end of the time period mentioned above. A request for representation does not relieve you of the obligation to file suit within this 90-day period.

This Notice should not be taken to mean that the Department of Justice has made a judgment as to whether or not your case is meritorious.

Sincerely,

Ralph F. Boyd, Jr.
Assistant Attorney General
Civil Rights Division

by Karen L. Ferguson
Civil Rights Analyst
Employment Litigation Section

cc: Jackson Area Office, EEOC
Marion County Sheriff's Dept.

Britton Mosley, Sr. & John Fancher

he Columbian-Progress

EEOC favors worker fired from prison

Despite a determination by the U.S. Equal Employment Opportunity Commission favoring the claim of a former Marion-Walthall Correctional Facility employee that his firing was retaliatory, an attorney representing the Marion County Sheriff's Department said the claim is without merit.

Britt Mosley Sr. was notified in October of 2001 that he had been terminated from his position as assistant chief of security at the correctional facility. Mosley said he was on administrative leave at the time.

A letter dated March 24 from the EEOC states Mosley claimed he was retaliated against because he filed a charge of discrimination against the sheriff's department on Jan. 5, 2001.

"I have determined that the evidence obtained in the investigation establishes reasonable cause to believe that (Mosley) was discriminated against...in that (he) was discharged on Oct. 30, 2001, while he was on a leave of absence approved by the Deputy Warden for the period Oct. 17, 2001, through November 2001," the letter states.

"The granting of this leave was as per the policies in effect at this time. The sheriff was not required to approve leave for employees in the correctional facility at that time. The policies which required him to approve leave became effective on Nov. 5, 2001. (Mosley) was already on leave under the old policies at that time."

Vicksburg attorney Ken Rector, who is representing the sheriff's office in cases arising from the firing of a number of employees at the correctional facility, said, however, that the EEOC's determination carries no legal weight.

"I don't expect there to be any change in our position," he said, noting that Mosley "was fired for not coming to work by (current warden) Joe Mingo, who is black. It's hard to make a racial discrimination complaint against another black man."

The letter from the EEOC points out, however, that "A white male was granted a verbal leave of absence in January, 2000. There is no evidence that there were any written records on this and no evidence that he was discharged."

Rector also questioned Mosley's contention that he was fired for filing a discrimination charge, citing the amount of time that passed between the time the complaint was filed in January and the time Mosley was fired at the end of October.

"If causation is there, it's usually a fairly short time period," he said.

If Mosley chooses to move ahead with his complaint, Rector said, the only option is to file suit in federal court.

Mosley said this week he intends either to file a new lawsuit, or to amend an existing one that claims he was subjected to a hostile work environment. Rector said a motion for summary judgment in that case is pending, and that he hopes to have a ruling on the motion within 60 days.

Mosley said his firing has had a "profound effect" on him.

"Personally, I feel a disservice was done to me there," he said. "It's caused tremendous hardships for me and my family."

Fabricating Evidence II

SERVING THE CITIZENS OF MARION COUNTY SINCE 1882

The Columbian-Progress

Saturday, August 2, 2003
COLUMBIA, MISSISSIPPI

Trial dates set for prison lawsuits

Trial dates have been set to hear lawsuits filed by two former employees of the Marion-Walthall Correctional Facility, who filed the federal lawsuits following their termination from the facility in October, 2001.

A trial in Southern District Court has been set for Britt Mosley Sr., assistant chief of security at the correctional facility at the time of his termination, on Feb. 4, 2004.

A trial has been set in the same court district for James Harvey Jr., who was deputy warden at the time of his firing, beginning April 26, 2004.

Mosley has claimed his firing was retaliatory because he had filed a charge of discrimination against the Marion County Sheriff's office earlier that year.

"I want the evidence to show the injustice I received at the hands of (Sheriff Richard) 'Rip' Stringer," Mosley said this week. "I think the evidence will speak for itself."

An attorney who is representing the sheriff's department in the cases said earlier that Mosley "was fired for not coming to work...," but a letter from the U.S. Equal Employment Opportunity Commission states an investigation by that agency showed "reasonable cause to believe..(Mosley) was discharged on Oct. 30, 2001, while he was on a leave of absence approved by the Deputy Warden for the period Oct. 17, 2001, through November 2001."

Stringer announced on Oct. 17, 2001 that Harvey and former Warden Jimmy Fancher had been relieved of their duties. A press release issued that day said the action was "based on administrative problems inside the facility," but both Harvey and Fancher disputed that allegation. Harvey said at the time he believed the action was retaliatory and, in his case, racial.

A month before the firings, representatives of the Marion County branch of the NAACP and the Marion County Civic Club had met with the Marion County Board of Supervisors to discuss complaints of alleged racial discrimination at the facility.

Harvey said this week he is looking forward to his case finally going to trial.

"I wish my court date were sooner," he said, adding, "I look forward to going to trial and letting the evidence show the real reason Sheriff Stringer fired me."

135

CHAPTER 7

Britton Mosley, Sr., versus Marion County Sheriff's Department

On November 7, 2001, the Britton Mosley, Sr., *versus* Marion County Sheriff's Department and Richard "Rip" Stringer lawsuit was filed in the United States District Court for the Southern District of Mississippi Jackson Division.

On March 18, 2003, former US District Judge Charles W. Pickering, Sr., recused himself from being the judge on my civil case against Marion County Sheriff's Department. Judge Pickering was the presiding judge in the case of Britton Mosley, Sr., *versus* Mississippi Department of Corrections. Compelling evidence shows that during that court proceeding, Judge Pickering gave unfair advantages to Mississippi Department of Corrections' personnel. After being traumatized by that rigged court proceeding, Mosley didn't expect to get a level playing field, seeking justice in the U.S. District Court for the Southern Division of Mississippi. This lawsuit would expose discrimination and corruption within the Marion County Sheriff's Department. Mosley endured verbal harassment, physical threats, and attempted conspiracy to plant illegal drugs on his possession. Evidence shows an ongoing situation of racism and injustice within the Marion County Sheriff's Department. Despite having two favorable Equal Employment Opportunity Commission determinations, Mosley didn't trust the judges in the U.S. District Courts for the Southern District of Mississippi. This distrust was motivated by the judicial misconduct at the hand of Judge Pickering's hostile attitude toward Mosley's case and other civil rights cases.

The late Judge L.T. Senter, Jr., was assigned to my discrimination lawsuit. Judge Senter was from Judge Pickering's generation, so there was a natural distrust for him. When Judge Senter granted the Defendant's Motion for Summary Judgement and dismissed Mosley lawsuit, Mosley wasn't surprised. Judge Senter overruled the Equal Employment Opportunity Commission's determination that the Marion County Sheriff's Department violated Title VIII of the Civil Rights Act of 1964. Mosley knew challenging this type of judicial bias was going to be an uphill battle, but he was up for the task. Judge Senter effectively disregarded the Equal Employment Opportunity Commission's finding; this is what white supremacy looks like in Mississippi. Mosley was very confused because he thought this was a thing of the past. This case showed the positions of power and influence were still largely owned and occupied disproportionately by white people.

Mosley appealed the District Court's grant of summary judgement, dismissing his suit in the United States Court of Appeals Fifth Circuit. The judgement of the district court was affirmed by the Fifth Circuit Court of Appeals.

Fabricating Evidence II

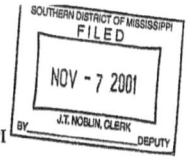

IN THE UNITED STATES DISTRICT COURT
FOR THE SOUTHERN DISTRICT OF MISSISSIPPI
JACKSON DIVISION

BRITTON MOSLEY, SR.   PLAINTIFF

VS.   NO. 3:01cv871LN

MARION COUNTY, MISSISSIPPI;
THE MARION COUNTY SHERIFF'S
DEPARTMENT; and RICHARD STRINGER,
in his official capacity as Sheriff of Marion County,
Mississippi   DEFENDANTS

<u>JURY DEMAND</u>

<u>COMPLAINT</u>

COMES NOW the Plaintiff, Britton Mosley and files this, his Complaint, for discrimination in violation of Title VII of the Civil Rights Act of 1964, 42 U.S.C. Section 2000, et. seq. and the Civil Rights Act of 1991, and intentional and/or negligent infliction of emotional harm, and violations of due process, pursuant to 42 U.S.C. Section 1983 in failing to follow established policies and procedures with regard to pay, and in support thereof will show unto the Court the following:

<u>PARTIES</u>

1. Plaintiff Britton Mosley is a Black adult resident citizen of Greene County, Mississippi.

2. Marion County, Mississippi is a political subdivision of the State of Mississippi. It is governed by a board of supervisors that is elected to oversee and manage the activities of Marion County, Mississippi. Marion County may be served by serving the President of the Marion County Board of Supervisors, Lloyd Ervin Fortenberry, at 250 Broad Street, Suite 2, Columbia, Mississippi 39429. Marion County, Mississippi is a covered employer under Title VII of the Civil Rights Act

of 1964, having more than twenty (20) employees.

3. The Marion County Sheriff's Department is a political subdivision of the State of Mississippi and Marion County, and may be served with process upon the Sheriff of Marion County, Mississippi, Richard Stringer, located at 503 South Main Street, Columbia, Mississippi 39429. Marion County, Mississippi is a covered employer under Title VII of the Civil Rights Act of 1964, having more than twenty (20) employees.

4. Defendant, Sheriff Richard Stringer, is an adult resident citizen of Marion County, Mississippi, and may be served with process upon his person at 503 South Main Street, Columbia, Mississippi 39429.

JURISDICTION

5. Jurisdiction of this Court is invoked pursuant to 28 U.S.C. Section 1331 and 1343.

FACTS

6. Plaintiff Mosley, a Black male, was hired by the Marion County Sheriff's Department in April 2000, and in February 2001, was promoted to assistant chief of security.

7. Beginning in February 2001, immediately after his promotion, Plaintiff Mosley was subjected to verbal harassment, physical threats, and attempted conspiracy to plant illegal drugs in his possession.

8. No reasons were given to Plaintiff Mosley for the above-referenced actions.

9. At all times material hereto, Plaintiff Mosley was qualified for the position of assistant chief of security.

10. Upon information and belief, Plaintiff Mosley was harassed and discriminated against because of his race, in an attempt to discredit him in his position.

Fabricating Evidence II

11. Additionally, Plaintiff Mosley was off work due to an injury, from December 18, 2000 until February 2001. Plaintiff Mosley was released to return to work on February 5, 2001. However, Plaintiff Mosley did not return to work until February 13, 2001, after requesting and being approved to use accumulated comp time to cover his leave, which was related to family matters, personal illness and jury duty.

12. On February 15, 2001, Plaintiff Mosley was only paid for two days of the applicable pay period.

13. When asked why Plaintiff Mosley only received two days' pay, the warden told him that it was docked because he did not have any comp time remaining.

14. Plaintiff Mosley's pay was docked in retaliation for filing a charge of discrimination against the Marion County Sheriff's Department.

15. The acts of discrimination and retaliation against the Plaintiff were intentional.

16. As a direct and proximate result of Defendants' discriminatory actions, the Plaintiff has suffered and will continue to suffer monetary as well as emotional losses.

17. On or about January 5, 2001, Plaintiff Mosley filed charges of discrimination with the Equal Employment Opportunity Commission based on racial discrimination. On or about February 26, 2001, Plaintiff Mosley amended his charge of discrimination. On or about August 11, 2001, Plaintiff Mosley received a Notice of Right to Sue which is attached hereto as Exhibit A.

CAUSES OF ACTION

COUNT I

18. Defendants' actions constituted unlawful discrimination in violation of Title VII of the Civil Rights Act of 1964, 42 U.S.C. § 2000e, et seq.

COUNT II

19. Defendants' actions constituted a violation of Plaintiff Mosley's substantive and procedural due process rights when they departed from the established policies and procedures to dock Plaintiff Mosley's pay. Therefore, the Defendants violated 42 U.S.C., Section 1983.

COUNT III

20. Defendants' actions constituted unlawful discrimination in violation of the Civil Rights Act of 1991.

COUNT IV

21. Defendants' actions constituted intentional and/or negligent infliction of emotional harm.

22. As a result of the Defendants' action, the Plaintiff was damaged in loss of pay, and in mental and emotional anguish and distress.

WHEREFORE, PREMISES CONSIDERED, the Plaintiff prays that this Complaint be filed and upon final hearing hereof, that this Court will grant Britton Mosley the following relief:

1. Any back pay owed.
2. Front pay, if necessary.
3. Compensatory damages in the amount not less than $75,000.00,
4. Reasonable attorneys fees and costs,

and such other general relief as this Court deems appropriate.

This the 7 day of November, 2001.

Respectfully submitted,

BRITTON MOSLEY

Fabricating Evidence II

BY: _____
HIAWATHA NORTHINGTON II, MSB # 10831

OF COUNSEL:

BYRD & ASSOCIATES
427 EAST FORTIFICATION STREET
POST OFFICE BOX 19
JACKSON, MISSISSIPPI 39205-0019
(601) 354-1210

Britton Mosley, Sr. & John Fancher

IN THE UNITED STATES DISTRICT COURT
FOR THE SOUTHERN DISTRICT OF MISSISSIPPI
HATTIESBURG DIVISION

BRITTON MOSLEY, SR.	PLAINTIFF(S)
VERSUS	CIVIL ACTION NO. 2:01CV310PG
MARION COUNTY, MS, et al.	DEFENDANT(S)

CASE MANAGEMENT ORDER

This order, including the deadlines established herein, having been established with the participation of all parties, can be modified only by order of the Court, and only upon a showing of good cause supported by affidavits, other evidentiary materials, or reference to portions of the record.

IT IS HEREBY ORDERED:

1. **CASE TRACK**

    This case is assigned to the standard track.

2. **ALTERNATE DISPUTE RESOLUTION**

    Alternative dispute resolution techniques may be helpful and may be used in this case.

3. **CONSENT TO TRIAL BY MAGISTRATE JUDGE**

    The parties do not consent to trial by a Magistrate Judge.

4. **DISCLOSURE**

    X   A.   The parties have fully complied with the initial disclosure requirements of the Plan.

        B.   The following additional disclosure is needed and is ordered as follows:

5. **MOTIONS AND ISSUE BIFURCATION**

    A.   It having been determined that the early filing of the following Motion(s) might significantly affect the scope of discovery or otherwise speed this

Fabricating Evidence II

matter along, it is ordered as follows:
Not applicable.

B. The Court determines that staged resolution, or bifurcation of the issues for trial consistent with Civil Rule 42(b) will assist in expediting this case. Accordingly, it is ordered as follows:
Not applicable.

6. **SPECIFIC DISCOVERY PROVISIONS OR LIMITATIONS**

Interrogatories, requests for production and requests for admissions should be limited to 30 succinct questions.

Depositions should be limited to the parties and no more than 5 fact witness depositions per party without prior approval of the Court.

ADDITIONAL DISCOVERY PROVISIONS OR LIMITATIONS

The Court finds that no further discovery provisions or limitations should be imposed.

7. **SCHEDULING DEADLINES**

TRIAL

ORDERED that this case is set for trial on May 5, 2003.

RESERVED TRIAL PERIOD (Two week limitation): Two weeks.

CONFLICTS: None reported.

(The Court will only consider conflicts specified in this CMO)

PRETRIAL

ORDERED that the pretrial conference in this case is set on April 4, 2003.

DISCOVERY

ORDERED that all discovery shall be completed on or before January 3, 2003.

Britton Mosley, Sr. & John Fancher

AMENDMENTS

ORDERED that Motions for joinder of parties or amendments to the pleadings shall be served on or before July 18, 2002.

EXPERTS

ORDERED that all the plaintiff's experts shall be designated on or before October 4, 2002.

ORDERED that all the defendant's experts shall be designated on or before November 4, 2002.

MOTIONS

ORDERED that all motions other than in limine motions shall be filed by January 17, 2003. The deadline for in limine motions is ten (10) days before the pretrial conference, with responses five (5) days before the pretrial conference.

SETTLEMENT CONFERENCE

ORDERED that a settlement conference shall be conducted by the appropriate judicial officer on December 13, 2002. If the parties unanimously agree that the conference will not be helpful, or that the parties should engage in mediation in lieu of a settlement conference, the parties shall contact the Chambers of the Magistrate Judge on or before November 13, 2002, to inform the Court that the conference is not necessary. If the parties do not contact the undersigned by November 13, 2002, the Court will provide notice of a time certain for the conference on December 13, 2002. In preparing for the settlement conference, the parties shall comply with Local Rule 16.1(C)(5) in submitting a settlement memorandum. In addition, the parties shall submit their settlement memorandum to U.S. District Judge Charles Pickering.

ORDERED this 20th day of June, 2002.

UNITED STATES MAGISTRATE JUDGE

Fabricating Evidence II

IN THE UNITED STATES DISTRICT COURT
SOUTHERN DISTRICT OF MISSISSIPPI
HATTIESBURG DIVISION

BRITTON MOSLEY, SR.   PLAINTIFF

VS.   CIVIL ACTION NO. 2:01cv310 PG

MARION COUNTY, MISSISSIPPI; THE MARION
COUNTY SHERIFF'S DEPARTMENT; AND RICHARD
STRINGER IN HIS OFFICIAL CAPACITY AS
SHERIFF OF MARION COUNTY, MISSISSIPPI   DEFENDANTS

DEFENDANT'S MOTION FOR SUMMARY JUDGMENT

COME NOW the Defendants, by their attorneys, and move the Court for summary judgment on all counts of the complaint filed herein against them, and in support of said motion would show unto the Court that there is no genuine issue of material fact and that Defendants are entitled to summary judgment as a matter of law on the following particular grounds:

1. Plaintiff has failed to establish a prima facie case of racial harassment or the existence of a racially hostile work environment.

2. Plaintiff has failed to present sufficient evidence that he was personally subjected to unwelcome harassment.

3. Plaintiff has failed to present sufficient evidence that he was personally harassed based on race.

4. Plaintiff has failed to present sufficient evidence that any conduct of Defendants directed to Plaintiff affected a term, condition or privilege of Plaintiff's employment.

5. Plaintiff has failed to present sufficient evidence that Defendants should have known of any alleged harassment and failed to take prompt remedial action.

6. Plaintiff has failed to present evidence to show that any alleged harassment was sufficiently severe or pervasive to create an abusive working environment.

7. Plaintiff has failed to present sufficient evidence to establish that Defendants are vicariously liable for any alleged harassment.

8. Plaintiff has failed to present sufficient evidence that Defendants' refusal to honor his demand for compensatory leave pay constituted an adverse employment action against the Plaintiff or that Defendants' refusal was causally connected to any activity by the Plaintiff protected by Title VII of the Civil Rights Act of 1964.

9. As a matter of law, Plaintiff's claim for compensatory leave pay does not involve an interest substantial enough to warrant protection of the Fourteenth Amendment and therefore Plaintiff does not state a cause of action under 42 USC §1983.

10. As a matter of law, Defendants are entitled to qualified immunity on Plaintiff's Section 1983 claim because Plaintiff has not provided sufficient evidence to demonstrate that refusal of Plaintiff's demand for compensatory leave pay violated a federal right that was clearly established at the time of such denial.

Defendants assign, in support of their motion, such other grounds as may be set forth in their Memorandum Brief of Authorities submitted herewith.

Defendants attach hereto in support of this motion excerpts from Plaintiff's deposition, and affidavits of Johnny Glover, Sheriff Richard Stringer and Catherine Williamson.

WHEREFORE, Defendants move the Court to grant them summary judgment on all counts of the complaint and to dismiss same with prejudice, assessing all costs to the Plaintiff.

Respectfully submitted,

MARION COUNTY, MISSISSIPPI; THE MARION COUNTY SHERIFF'S DEPARTMENT; AND RICHARD STRINGER IN HIS OFFICIAL CAPACITY AS SHERIFF OF MARION COUNTY, MISSISSIPPI

BY: _____
Kenneth B. Rector
Bar No. 4681

CERTIFICATE

I, Kenneth B. Rector, do hereby certify that I have this day mailed, postage prepaid, a true and correct copy of the above and foregoing to Hiawatha Northington, II, Byrd & Associates, P. O. Box 19, Jackson, MS 39205-0019.

THIS 10 day of January, 2003.

_____
KENNETH B. RECTOR

Britton Mosley, Sr. & John Fancher

NORTHINGTON LAW FIRM

PHYSICAL ADDRESS:

802 NORTH ST.
JACKSON, MS 39202

PHONE: 601.914.0248
FAX: 601.914.0255

HIAWATHA NORTHINGTON II*

MAILING ADDRESS:

P.O. BOX 1003
JACKSON, MS 39215-1003

*LICENSED IN: MISSISSIPPI, TEXAS

January 30, 2004

Britton Mosley
P.O. Box 390
State Line, MS 39362

    RE: Mosley v. Marion County, MS
             Civil Action No. 2:01cv310PG

Dear Britt:

I hate to be the bearer of bad news, but I have enclosed a copy of an opinion that I received from Judge Senter today. He has granted the Defendants' Motion for Summary Judgment after all this time, and has dismissed this particular lawsuit.

I will be filing an appeal for you in this matter (assuming that you want me to) next week, because I think that he erred in two ways: 1) he concluded that there were no material facts present to suggest that you were in a hostile work environment, basically stating that he gave more credence to Johnnie Glover's affidavit than James Harvey's affidavit; and 2) he concluded that there was not a genuine issue of material fact as to your retaliation claim, effectively disregarding the EEOC finding.

I would also suggest at this time that you go ahead and request your right to sue letter from the EEOC on your outstanding charge related to your termination, so that I may go ahead and file that lawsuit.

I will have spoken to you before you get this letter. Again, I am sorry to have to give you this information, much less since it's so late in the game. I know how bad you want this, and this is definitely not the end. I am also sending a copy of the opinion to James Harvey. Thank you very much for your attention to this matter.

Very truly yours,

NORTHINGTON LAW FIRM

Hiawatha Northington II
Hiawatha Northington II

Encl.

cc: James Harvey (w/encl)

Fabricating Evidence II

IN THE UNITED STATES DISTRICT COURT
SOUTHERN DISTRICT OF MISSISSIPPI
HATTIESBURG DIVISION

BRITTON MOSLEY, SR.   PLAINTIFF

VS.   CIVIL ACTION NO. 2:01cv310 SRo

MARION COUNTY, MISSISSIPPI; THE MARION
COUNTY SHERIFF'S DEPARTMENT; AND RICHARD
STRINGER IN HIS OFFICIAL CAPACITY AS
SHERIFF OF MARION COUNTY, MISSISSIPPI   DEFENDANTS

NOTICE OF APPEAL

By this notice, the Plaintiff, Britton Mosley, appeals to the United States Court of Appeals for the Fifth Circuit, from that Memorandum Opinion and Order signed on January 30, 2004 and entered in this cause on February 2, 2004.

This 26 day of February, 2004.

Respectfully submitted,

/s/ Hiawatha Northington II
HIAWATHA NORTHINGTON II, MSB # 10831

OF COUNSEL:

NORTHINGTON LAW FIRM
802 NORTH STREET (39202)
P.O. BOX 1003
JACKSON, MS 39215-1003
601.914.0248

Britton Mosley, Sr. & John Fancher

CERTIFICATE OF SERVICE

I, Hiawatha Northington II, one of the attorneys for the Plaintiff, hereby certify that I have this day served a true and correct copy of the above and foregoing document via United States Mail, postage prepaid, on the following:

Kenneth B. Rector
Wheeless Shappley Bailess & Rector, LLP
P.O. Box 991
Vicksburg, MS 39181-0991

Hon. L.T. Senter, Jr.
United States District Court
2012 15th Street, Suite 514
Gulfport, MS 39501

This the 26 day of February, 2004.

_____
HIAWATHA NORTHINGTON II

Fabricating Evidence II

United States Court of Appeals
Fifth Circuit

F I L E D

October 5, 2004

UNITED STATES COURT OF APPEALS
FIFTH CIRCUIT

Charles R. Fulbruge III
Clerk

No. 04-60192

(Summary Calendar)

BRITTON MOSLEY, SR,

           Plaintiff - Appellant,

versus

MARION COUNTY, MISSISSIPPI; MARION COUNTY SHERIFF'S DEPARTMENT; RICHARD STRINGER, In his official capacity as Sheriff of Marion County, Mississippi,

           Defendants - Appellees.

Appeal from the United States District Court
For the Southern District of Mississippi
USDC No. 2:01-CV-310-SRO

Before EMILIO M. GARZA, DeMOSS, and CLEMENT, Circuit Judges.

PER CURIAM:[*]

    Appellant, Britton Mosley, Sr., appeals the district court's grant of summary judgment dismissing his suit for employment discrimination and retaliation under Title VII of the Civil Rights

---

[*] Pursuant to 5TH CIR. R. 47.5, the court has determined that this opinion should not be published and is not precedent except under the limited circumstances set forth in 5TH CIR. R. 47.5.4.

Act of 1964 and for relief under 42 U.S.C. § 1983.

We review the district court's order granting summary judgment *de novo*. *Melton v. Teachers Inc. & Annuity Ass'n of America*, 114 F.3d 557, 559 (5th Cir. 1997). Summary judgment is proper if the pleadings, depositions, answers to interrogatories, and admissions on file, together with any affidavits filed in support of the motion, show that there is no genuine issue as to any material fact and that the moving party is entitled to judgment as a matter of law. FED. R. CIV. P. 56(c). In reviewing the record, we do so in the light most favorable to the non-moving party and the non-moving party is entitled to all reasonable inferences that may be drawn from the facts. *Anderson v. Liberty Lobby, Inc.*, 477 U.S. 242, 255 (1986).

Mosley alleges hostile work environment and race discrimination claiming he was subjected to verbal harassment, physical threats, and attempted conspiracy to plant illegal drugs in his possession. In order to prove a prima facie hostile work environment claim, Mosley must establish five essential elements: (1) the employee belongs to the protected group; (2) the employee was subjected to unwelcome harassment; (3) the harassment complained of was based on race; (4) the harassment complained of affected a term, condition, or privilege of employment; (5) the employer knew or should have known of the harassment in question and failed to take prompt remedial action. *See Watts v. Kroger Co.*, 170 F.3d 505, 509 (5th Cir. 1999). In order for harassment to affect a term, condition or privilege of employment, it must be "sufficiently severe or pervasive so as to alter the conditions of employment and create an abusive working environment." *Id.* at 510.

Mosley identified eight incidents that he contends—considered together—created a hostile work environment. After reviewing the record and briefs submitted by the parties, we agree with the district court's analysis and finding that there is no admissible evidence sufficient to create a genuine issue of material fact in support of the plaintiff's claims. Mosley's claims are either supported by no admissible evidence, no evidence to refute that offered by the defendant, or no evidence offered to demonstrate that defendants' actions were racially motivated. Mosley has, however, offered evidence of three incidents involving the use of racial slurs. We agree, however, with the district court's conclusion that these claims alone are insufficient to establishing a general issue of material fact for Mosley's hostile work environment claim under Title VII.

Mosley also alleges that his pay was docked as retaliation for having filed a complaint with the EEOC, charging that he was not paid for accumulated, unused compensatory leave for the pay period ending February 15, 2001. When Mosley returned to work his pay resumed at its normal rate for the last seven months of his employment. "In order to prove a prima facie case in a retaliation claim the employee must show: (1) that the employee engaged in activity protected by Title VII; (2) the employer took adverse employment action against the employee; and (3) a causal connection exists between the protected activity and the adverse employment action." *Haynes v. Pennzoil Company*, 207 F.3d 296, 299 (5th Cir. 2000). In order to prevail on his retaliation claim, Mosley thus had to demonstrate that Appellees had no justification for reducing his pay for the period ending February 15, 2001. As the district court noted, there is no evidence in the record to contradict Catherine Williamson's affidavit stating that Mosley's accumulated compensation time was exhausted, thus establishing a non-discriminatory and non-retaliatory reason for the decrease in Mosley's pay for the pay period ending February 15, 2001. The EEOC determination alone is not sufficient to contradict Appellee's non-discriminatory reason for Mosley's decrease in pay. *Price v. Federal Express Corp.*, 283 F.3d 715, 725 (5th Cir. 2002). Thus, we affirm the District Court's determination that there is no genuine issue of material fact in support of plaintiff's retaliation claim.

Britton Mosley, Sr. & John Fancher

Accordingly, the judgment of the district court is AFFIRMED.

CHAPTER 8

The Mississippi State Conference of the NAACP's Investigation

During a press conference in Jackson, Mississippi, the Mississippi State Conference of the Mississippi State Conference of the NAACP stated its investigation into the Marion/Walthall Correctional Facility had relevance to its opposition of Judge Charles W. Pickering's nomination to the Fifth Circuit.

On July 20, 2001, there was a state investigation of Marion/Walthall Correctional Facility conducted by the State Attorney General's Office. According to former Attorney General Mike Moore's office, the state investigator assigned to investigate Marion/Walthall Correctional Facility was identified as Roger Cribbs. During an interview Cribbs had with Marion/Walthall Correctional Facility's Major Johnny Glover, an audio tape was secretly recording that meeting. Graphic, sexual comments and racial slurs were made. In addition, present at that meeting were Chief Deputy Rocky Williamson and Detective Tim Singly of the Marion County Sheriff's Department. There are allegations that Mississippi Department of Corrections Investigator Tim Wilson was also present.

Lee Martin, Assistant Attorney General, confirmed that an agency investigator was present during the conversation, but the investigator didn't make a racial comment. The late L.A. Warren, head of the Legal Redress Division of the Mississippi State Conference of the NAACP, said Martin told him in August that a Mississippi Department of Corrections employee was present at the meeting. Warren said, "I'm receiving conflicting information. The first time they met, they should have known who was there. It should have been consistent from day one." One could only assume they had the facts and they were trying to cover them up. The State Mississippi State Conference of the NAACP met with former Attorney General Mike Moore and Mississippi Department of Corrections officials about the audio recording. Both state agencies deny one of its investigators made an inappropriate remark.

The first voice on the tape clearly says, "This is a state investigation and if anybody talks about this, they can be charged."

Having been interviewed by Attorney General's Investigator Roger Cribb, Mosley recognized his voice as the person making that statement. Cribb's voice can be heard throughout the audio recording, making graphic, racial, and sexual comments.

On January 31, 2002, the Mississippi State Conference of the Mississippi State Conference of the NAACP called a press conference to release a series of audio tapes that shows the continuing conspiracy between local, state, and federal officials to cover-up and prolong the instances of longstanding civil rights violations.

On July 20, 2001, there was a state investigation of the Marion/Walthall Correctional Facility conducted by the Attorney General's Office. According to Attorney General Mike Moore's office, the state investigator assigned to investigate Marion/Walthall Correctional Facility was verified as Roger Cribbs.

Mr. Cribbs was interviewing Major Johnny Glover of Marion/Walthall Correctional Facility. Others present at this interview, according to the Attorney General's Office, were Chief Deputy Rocky Williamson and Detective Tim Singley. It appears that Glover, Williamson, and Singley made racial slurs, too.

The racial slurs continued with Roger Cribbs using the old racial slur: "I'd rather be red on the head like the dick of a dog than brown on the crown like shit on the ground."

Investigator Cribbs racially profiled former African American Assistant Warden James Harvey and all other African American officers at Unit 29 at Parchman Prison as being "gang bangers" when he stated, "That's not out of the ordinary though for them."

Investigator Cribbs used double standards when interviewing whites and African Americans. When interviewing whites, the process was done collectively and not recorded. However, when interviewing African Americans, it was individually and recorded.

The Marion/Walthall Correctional Facility is a county-owned facility that houses state inmates. There appears to be a pattern of conspiracy and cover-up involving Mississippi Department of Corrections and the Attorney General's Office. Mississippi Department of Corrections claims that they are unaware of who was present at this investigation of Marion/Walthall Correctional Facility.

Shortly after the racial profiling audio tape was exposed, the Attorney General's Office and the Mississippi Department of Corrections investigation were completed. The Mississippi State

Conference of the NAACP sent former Mississippi Attorney General Mike Moore a formal request to begin a second investigation in connection with activities at Marion/Walthall Correctional Facility. The Attorney General's Office confirmed it had received a request on behalf of the Mississippi State Conference of the NAACP to investigate the Marion County Sheriff's Department concerning allegations involving the facility. The letter was signed by late L.A. Warren, Chairman of the Legal Redress Committee of the Mississippi State Conference of the NAACP. Mr. Warren asked the Attorney General's Office to look into a number of allegations, including that Sheriff Stringer allegedly made false allegations to cause the investigation into the regional facility.

During a meeting at the Mississippi Rural Center in Lampton Community, Warren said formal complaints would be filed with the offices of the State Attorney General and the U.S. Department of Justice. The attached evidence shows the Attorney General's Office investigations were racially and politically biased. There was a disturbing pattern of discrimination in Marion County. During the Attorney General's initial investigation, the office indicted and prosecuted a former Marion/Walthall Correctional Facility employer, an African American male, for falsifying a travel expense voucher. However, the Attorney General's Office received evidence that a white female nurse at Marion/Walthall Correctional Facility was caught by a correctional officer having sex with a state inmate in the facility's infirmary, a violation of State Statue 97-3-104, and no charges were brought against the nurse. Special Assistant Attorney General Lee Martin said the nurse's conduct does not constitute a violation of MCA 97-3-104 (Rev. 2000). Martin also stated the Attorney General's Office does not engage in selective prosecution. However, an African American female correctional officer at the Central Mississippi Correctional Facility in Pearl, Mississippi, accused of having sex with an inmate was arrested and indicted.

The Mississippi State Conference of the NAACP and Attorney General's Office never informed Jimmy Fancher and Britton Mosley, Sr., whether or not a second requested Attorney General's investigation be conducted. The Mississippi State Conference of the NAACP and the Attorney General's Office never provided any information concerning the second investigation request.

The evidence in this chapter shows the Mississippi Attorney General's investigations prosecutions are racially and politically selective. The Attorney General's Office condoned corruption by staff members within the Mississippi Department of Corrections and the Marion/Walthall Correctional Facility. The Mississippi State Conference of the NAACP never gave Fancher and Mosley a reason as to why the Attorney General's Office did not conduct a second investigation, which was a painful disappointment.

Britton Mosley, Sr. & John Fancher

NATIONAL ASSOCIATION FOR THE ADVANCEMENT OF COLORED PEOPLE
MISSISSIPPI STATE CONFERENCE

EUGENE BRYANT
President

Katherine Egland
1st Vice-President

Melvin Hollins
2nd Vice-President

Emma Sims
3rd Vice-President

Eric Cook
4th Vice-President

Curley Clark
5th Vice-President

Doris Smith
6th Vice-President

Timothy Jackson
7th Vice-President

Gwendolyn E. Holmes
Treasurer

Janette Self
Secretary

Dorothy Isaac
Assistant Secretary

MS Attorney General
Mike Moore
P. O. Box 220
Jackson MS 39205

Dear Mike:

This is the formal request that Mr. Martin said had to be filed to request a formal and full investigation of the Marion County Sheriff Department.

Allegation: 1. Sheriff Richard Stringer of the Marion County Sheriff's Department made false allegations or sworn statements to cause an investigation against Deputy Warden James Harvey of the Marion Walthall Correctional Facility. It appear a violation of State statute 97-7-37 has been committee.

    2. Chief Deputy Rocky Williamson did knowingly and willfully on December 28, 2000 conspire to fabricate and entrap Deputy Warden Harvey on false drug changes with the consent of Sheriff Richard Stringer.

    3. Chief Deputy Rocky Williamson did knowingly and willfully on or about April of 2000 accept an unauthorized fee and introduce contraband into the Marion Walthall Correctional Facility in Columbia Ms.

    4. There appears to be a pattern of conspiracy, violations of color of law and entrapment perpetrated by the Marion County Sheriff's Department.

We are seeking a full and complete investigation from your office with a written report of the findings.

Thanking you in advance:

L A Warren
Chairman Legal Redress Committee

CC: Eugene Bryant
    President MS State Conference

    Attorney Dennis Hayes
    National General Council

    Mrs. Floree Smith
    Marion County President

1072 West Lynch Street • Suite 10 • Jackson, Mississippi 39203 • (601) 353-6906 • 1-800-80NAACP • FAX (601) 353-1565

Fabricating Evidence II

NATIONAL ASSOCIATION FOR THE ADVANCEMENT OF COLORED PEOPLE
MISSISSIPPI STATE CONFERENCE

For Immediate Release: January 31, 2002

For more information, contact: L. A. Warren
Legal Redress
Committee Chair
(601) 353-6906

EUGENE BRYANT, SR.
President

George Roberts
1st Vice President

Curley Clark
2nd Vice President

Melvin Hollins
3rd Vice President

Derrick Johnson
4th Vice President

Kelvin Buck
5th Vice President

Eddie Smith
6th Vice President

Janette Self
Secretary

Dorothy Isaac
Asst. Secretary

James Crowell
Treasurer

James Creer
Asst. Treasurer

PRESS STATEMENT

January 31, 2002—The Mississippi State Conference of the NAACP calls this press conference to release the second in a series of audio tapes that will show the continuing conspiracy between local, state, and federal officials to cover-up and prolong the instances of longstanding civil rights violations.

On July 20, 2001, there was a state investigation of the Marion-Walthall Correctional Facility conducted by the AG's office. According to Attorney General Mike Moore's office, the state investigator assigned to investigate the MWCF was identified as Roger Cribbs. Mr. Cribbs was interviewing Major Johnnie Glover of the MWCF.

Others present at this interview, according to the AG's office, were Chief Deputy Rocky Williamson and Detective Tim Singley. Investigator Cribbs stated that this interview was part of a state criminal investigation, "and if anyone talked about it, they could be charged."

Investigator Cribbs then proceeded to make a graphic sexual comment too obscene to print. It appears that Major Johnny Glover made a racial slur, as well. It also appears that either Chief Deputy Rocky Williamson or Detective Tim Singley made racial slurs, too.

The racial slurs also continued with Roger Cribbs, using the old racial slur that says, "I'd rather be red on the head like the dick of a dog, than brown on the crown like shit on the ground."

Investigator Cribbs racially profiled former black Deputy Warden James Harvey and all other black officers at Unit 29 at Parchman prison as being "gang bangers" when he stated, "that's not out of the ordinary though for them."

We are waiting for the AG's explanation as to why Chief Deputy Rocky Williamson and Detective Tim Singley of the Marion County Sheriff's Department were present at the interview of the investigation of MWCF by Roger Cribbs. We are also waiting on the AG's report of the investigation of the prior allegations of misconduct made by

1072 West Lynch Street • Suite 10 • Jackson, Mississippi 39203 • (601) 353-6906 • 1-800-80NAACP • FAX (601) 353-1565

Page 2
NAACP Press Statement
January 31, 2002

the NAACP against Sheriff Rip Stringer and Chief Deputy Rocky Williamson. We are also awaiting Investigator Roger Cribbs' explanation as to *why* he can't remember *who* said *what* and *why* the interview was not recorded.

It appears that Agent Cribbs uses double standards when interviewing whites and blacks. When interviewing whites, the process was done collectively and not recorded; however, when interviewing blacks, it was individually and recorded.

The web of conspiracy appears to evolve from the Marion County Sheriff's Office to possibly, the federal bench.

On December 28, 2000, there was a failed attempt of entrapment against former Deputy Warden James Harvey by Marion County Sheriff Richard "Rip" Stringer and Chief Deputy Rocky Williamson. *(See tape and transcript)*

The Marion-Walthall Correctional Facility is a county owned facility that houses state inmates. There appears to be a pattern of conspiracy and cover-up involving Mississippi Department of Corrections and the AG's office. The MDOC *claims* that they are unaware of who was present at this investigation of MWCF.

The NAACP investigation reveals that Captain Britton Mosley, Sr., who was fired from Marion/Walthall Correctional Facility, appears to have also been a victim of an earlier drug setup and conspiracy by MDOC, the AG's office, and a federal judge.

Drugs were planted on Mosley by former staff member Michael Miller at South Mississippi Correctional Institution, who hired then-attorney Keith Miller, who is now District Attorney for Jackson, George and Green counties. Upon Miller becoming District Attorney, he dismissed the charges on his client without prejudice. When affidavits in the case were filed, he promised to appoint a special prosecutor—which never occurred.

Approximately a month ago, Mississippi State Conference NAACP Second Vice-President Curley Clark took eleven affidavits back to District Attorney Miller, who told him he would again appoint a special prosecutor; to our knowledge, this has not occurred.

The Attorney General's office also failed or refused to investigate the Mosley case. From this inaction, Mosley filed a lawsuit in U.S. District Court. The case was presided over by Federal Judge Charles W. Pickering, Sr.

Before hearing the case, Judge Pickering ordered a state agency to investigate another state agency—instead of asking the FBI (a federal agency) to investigate Mosley's

NAACP questions AG probe into correctional facility

Alleges connection by Judge Pickering

During a press conference in Jackson Thursday, the Mississippi State Conference of the NAACP said its investigation into the Marion-Walthall Correctional Facility has relevance to its opposition of Judge Charles W. Pickering's nomination to the Fifth Circuit.

"On July 20, 2001, there was a state investigation of the Marion-Walthall Correctional Facility conducted by the (state Attorney General's) office," the NAACP's announcement states. "According to Attorney General Mike Moore's office, the state investigator assigned to investigate the MWCF was identified as Roger Cribbs. Mr. Cribbs was interviewing Major Johnnie Glover of the MWCF."

A tape secretly made of that meeting includes a graphic sexual comment and racial slurs. The NAACP had earlier asked state officials to look into the incident.

"We are waiting for the AG's explanation as to why Chief Deputy Rocky Williamson and Detective Tim Singley of the Marion County Sheriff's Department were present at the interview of the investigation of MWCF by Roger Cribbs," Thursday's announcement states. "We are also waiting on the AG's report of the investigation of the prior allegations of misconduct made by the NAACP against Sheriff "Rip" Stringer and Chief Deputy Rocky Williamson. We are also awaiting Investigator Roger Cribbs' explanation as to why he can't remember who said what and why the interview was not (officially) recorded."

The NAACP also alleges that a chain of events involving Captain Britton Mosley Sr., who was fired from the Marion-Walthall Correctional Facility, along with the warden and assistant warden, includes involvement by Pickering.

Mosley has alleged that, while earlier employed at South Mississippi Correctional Institution in Green County, drugs were planted on him by a former staff member. That employee was represented by attorney Keith Miller, who is now District Attorney for Jackson, George and Green Counties.

"Upon Miller becoming District Attorney, he dismissed the charges on his client without prejudice," the announcement states. "When affidavits in the case were filed, he promised to appoint a special prosecutor — which never occurred."

The statement continues, "The Attorney General's office also failed or refused to investigate the Mosley case. From this inaction, Mosley filed a lawsuit in U.S. District Court. The case was presided over by Federal Judge Charles W. Pickering Sr. Before hearing the case, Judge Pickering ordered a state agency to investigate another state agency — instead of asking the FBI (a federal agency) to investigate Mosley's allegations...Judge Pickering's bias was so evident that he even ordered a background check on Mosley — just as he did in the early 1970s, when he asked the Sovereignty Commission to do a background check on the organizers of the pulpwood haulers union in Laurel, Miss."

JAIL DOCKET

Page 7A
Thursday, July 10, 2003
E-mail: news@columbianprogress.com

NAACP has questions about prison

An official with the state NAACP who had requested the state Attorney General's office to look into the operation of the Marion/Walthall Correctional Facility in 2001 is continuing to seek a response to that request, as well as bringing new concerns to the attention of that office.

In a letter to the Attorney General's office dated June 9, L.A. Warren, legal redress chairman with the Mississippi State Conference of the National Association for the Advancement of Colored People, stated that the NAACP had yet to receive a written response to the request made in 2001.

"Because of the considerable time that has lapsed since the filing of the complaint, you can understand our concern," the letter states.

The Attorney General's office responded in a letter dated June 13 that it had provided a letter in April concerning its investigation, but Warren said the April letter did not address the concerns mentioned in his June 9 letter and has asked for an additional response.

Warren also wrote that, "There also seems to be another disturbing pattern developing in Marion County. During your initial investigation, your office indicted and prosecuted a former employee, Charles Evans, a black male, for falsifying a travel expense voucher. Well, we have received information that a white female...who was employed as a nurse at the Marion County facility was caught on April 21, 2003 by a corrections officer (allegedly) having sex with a state inmate in the facility infirmary."

The letter continues that, "At the time of this letter, we know of no charges having been brought against (the former employee) either by the Marion County Sheriff's office or your office. This type of selective prosecution of persons at the Marion County facility concerns us greatly."

In its June 13 letter, the Attorney General's office responded, however that, "the conduct does not constitute a violation" of the state code. The nurse, who is no longer employed at the facility "is not employed in one of the positions listed in that statute," the letter continues. "Thus, she could not be charged with a violation of such statute. Furthermore, I am not aware of any other criminal statute which would be applicable to the situation."

Although the sheriff's department reportedly investigated the incident, Sheriff Richard "Rip" Stringer has declined to comment on the situation, which he said was a personnel matter.

Fabricating Evidence II

The Columbian-Progress

50 cents

AG completes investigation of prison

'Questionable practices' uncovered at facility

By Dann Gower
Staff Writer

An investigation by the state Attorney General's office of the Marian Walthall Correctional Facility is complete, and the results are expected to be turned over to the state Department of Corrections for possible action.

the Attorney General's office reported Tuesday.

Representatives of the Attorney General's office and the state Corrections Department met Tuesday morning with officers of the state NAACP to discuss the investigation and concerns the NAACP had with the way it was conducted.

"It appears to us it was politically motivated," L.A. Warren, chairman of the Legal Redress Committee of the state NAACP, said of the investigation, which was reportedly made at the request of the Marion County Sheriff's Department. Warren said it was his understanding that no major infraction on the part of those running the facility turned up as a result of the investigation, although he said some changes may be made in the use of inmate labor in the future.

Lee Martin, a special assistant attorney general, however, said the investigation turned up questionable practices on the part of both employees and inmates at the facility, including "potentially a felony charge."

Warren said the meeting cleared up his concerns about the actions of the Attorney General's office in connection with that agency's investigation into the facility, but said he still wants sharper direction for the investigation.

One question that still remained following the meeting was the identity of a person who was taped making racial slurs during the investigation, Warren said.

adding that the Attorney General's office has said it will ask its investigator to identify to be made the information during a meeting the investigator attended.

"We have told them unequivocally that our investigators did not make those comments," Martin said following the meeting.

See Prison, Page 2

Prison...From Page 1

Warren said the NAACP plans to file a complaint concerning the person responsible since the organization learns who made the comments.

Warren had also warned of the rights of prisoners at the facility that have been violated during the investigation, a charge that was disputed by the Attorney General's office.

There was no indication of an inmate's rights, Martin said following the meeting. Warren said there is a possibility that the inmate who were transferred to other facilities during the investigation may be returned to the Marian Walthall facility.

Since October, three top level prison officials have been fired by Marion County Sheriff Ed Baird, including the former warden and associate warden.

The Columbian-Progress

Second AG investigation requested at prison

Former employee claims conspiracy to plant drugs

A formal request has been sent to the state Attorney General's office to begin a second investigation in the Marion/Walthall Correctional Facility, that office confirmed this week.

The Attorney General's office had earlier confirmed, but refused to comment about, an ongoing investigation at the correctional facility. A letter Marion County Sheriff Richard "Rip" Stringer wrote to former warden Jimmy Fancher states that Stringer initiated that investigation based on "complaints and allegations that I had received" about activities at the facility.

The Attorney General's office received a request on behalf of the NAACP to investigate the sheriff's office concerning allegations involving the facility.

The letter, signed by L.A.

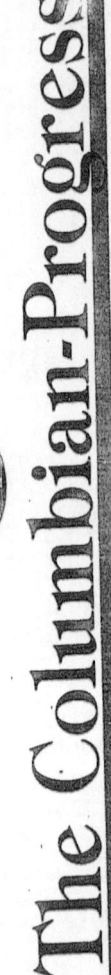

L.A. Warren

Warren, chairman of the Legal Redress Committee of the state NAACP, asks the Attorney General's office to look into a number of allegations, including that Stringer allegedly made false allegations to cause the investigation into the regional facility.

During a meeting held last month at the Mississippi Rural Center in the Lampton community, Warren said formal complaints would be filed with the offices of the state Attorney General and the U.S. Department of Justice.

The NAACP's request comes on the heels of a lawsuit filed in the Southern District of U.S. District Court on Nov. 7 on behalf of Britton "Britt" Mosley Sr., the former assistant chief of security at the facility, against Marion County, the Marion County Sheriff's Department and Richard Stringer in his official capacity as sheriff of Marion County.

According to that suit, "Beginning in February 2001, immediately after his promotion, plaintiff Mosley was subjected to verbal harassment, physical threats and attempted conspiracy to plant illegal drugs in his possession."

The suit continues, "On or about Jan. 5, 2001, plaintiff Mosley filed charges of discrimination with the Equal Employment Opportunity Commission based on racial discrimination. On or about Feb. 26, 2001, plaintiff Mosley amended his charge of discrimination. On or about Aug. 11, 2001, plaintiff Mosley received a notice of right to sue..."

Mosley's suit requests any back pay owed, front pay (if necessary), compensatory damages of not less than $75,000, reasonable attorneys fees and costs and general relief deemed appropriate by the court.

The Columbian-Progress

Thursday, November 24, 2001 — 50 cents

AG completes investigation of prison

'Questionable practices' uncovered at facility

By Dana Gower
Staff Writer

An investigation by the state Attorney General's office of the Marion Waldhall Correctional Facility is complete, and the results are expected to be turned over to the state Department of Corrections for possible action.

the Attorney General's office reported Tuesday.

Representatives of the Attorney General's office and the state corrections department met Tuesday morning with officers of the state NAACP to discuss the investigation and concerns the NAACP had with the way it was conducted.

"It appears to us it was politically motivated," L.A. Warren, chairman of the Legal Redress Committee of the state NAACP, said of the investigation, which was reportedly made at the request of the Marion County Sheriff's Department. Warren said it was his understanding that no major infractions on the part of those running the facility turned up as a result of the investigation, although he said some changes may be made in the use of inmate labor in the future.

Lee Martin, a special assistant attorney general, said, however, that the investigation turned up questionable practices on the part of both employees and inmates at the facility, including potentially a felony charge.

Warren said the meeting cleared up his concerns about the actions of the Attorney General's office in connection with that agency's investigation into the facility, but said he still has concerns about the reason for the investigation.

One question that still remained following the meeting was the identity of a person who was rapped making racial slurs during the investigation, Warren said,

adding that the Attorney General's office has said it will ask its investigator to identify who made the comment during a meeting the investigator attended.

"We have told them unequivocally that our investigators did not make those comments," Martin said following the meeting.

See Prison, Page 2

Prison...From Page 1

Warren said the NAACP plans to file a complaint concerning the person responsible since the organization learns who made the comments.

Warren had also accused the facility of mistreatment of the rights of prisoners at the facility may have been violated during the investigation, a charge that was disputed by the Attorney General's office.

There was no evidence of any inmate's rights, Martin said following the meeting.

Warren said there is a possibility that the inmates who were

transferred to other facilities during the investigation may be returned to the Marion Waldhall facility.

Since October, three top level prison officials have been fired by Marion County Sheriff Richard "Rip" Strange, including the former warden and assistant warden

JAIL DOCKET

NAACP has questions about prison

An official with the state NAACP who had requested the state Attorney General's office to look into the operation of the Marion/Walthall Correctional Facility in 2001 is continuing to seek a response to that request, as well as bringing new concerns to the attention of that office.

In a letter to the Attorney General's office dated June 9, L.A. Warren, legal redress chairman with the Mississippi State Conference of the National Association for the Advancement of Colored People, stated that the NAACP had yet to receive a written response to the request made in 2001.

"Because of the considerable time that has lapsed since the filing of the complaint, you can understand our concern," the letter states.

The Attorney General's office responded in a letter dated June 13 that it had provided a letter in April concerning its investigation, but Warren said the April letter did not address the concerns mentioned in his June 9 letter and has asked for an additional response.

Warren also wrote that, "There also seems to be another disturbing pattern developing in Marion County. During your initial investigation, your office indicted and prosecuted a former employee, Charles Evans, a black male, for falsifying a travel expense voucher. Well, we have received information that a white female...who was employed as a nurse at the Marion County facility was caught on April 21, 2003 by a corrections officer (allegedly) having sex with a state inmate in the facility infirmary."

The letter continues that, "At the time of this letter, we know of no charges having been brought against (the former employee) either by the Marion County Sheriff's office or your office. This type of selective prosecution of persons at the Marion County facility concerns us greatly."

In its June 13 letter, the Attorney General's office responded, however that, "the conduct does not constitute a violation" of the state code. The nurse, who is no longer employed at the facility "is not employed in one of the positions listed in that statute, the letter continues. Thus, she could not be charged with a violation of such statute. Furthermore, I am not aware of any other criminal statute which would be applicable to the situation." Although the sheriff's department reportedly investigated the incident, Sheriff Richard "Rip" Stringer has declined to comment on the situation, which he said was a personnel matter.

Page 7A
Thursday, July 10, 2003
E-mail: news@columbianprogress.com

Fabricating Evidence II

STATE OF MISSISSIPPI
OFFICE OF THE ATTORNEY GENERAL

MIKE MOORE
ATTORNEY GENERAL

PUBLIC INTEGRITY
DIVISION

April 5, 2002

Mr. L.A. Warren
1072 West Lynch Street, Suite 10
Jackson, MS. 39203

Dear Mr. Warren:

    Copies of the investigative file concerning the Marion-Walthall Correctional Facility are enclosed. We have redacted names of certain informants and other witnesses who provided information during the course of the investigation. This was done of course to protect their identity and to ensure that in the future others will cooperate in our investigations without fear of their names being disclosed. Thank you.

Lee Martin
Special Assistant Attorney General

/lm

802 N. STATE STREET • P. O. BOX 2 • JACKSON, MS 39205-0002
TELEPHONE (601) 359-4250 • FAX (601) 359-4254

173

Second AG investigation requested at prison

Former employee claims conspiracy to plant drugs

A formal request has been sent to the state Attorney General's office to begin a second investigation in connection with activities at the Marion-Walthall Correctional Facility, that office confirmed this week.

The Attorney General's office had earlier confirmed, but refused to comment about, an ongoing investigation at the correctional facility. A letter Marion County Sheriff Richard "Rip" Stringer wrote to former warden Jimmy Fancher states that Stringer initiated that investigation based on "complaints and allegations that I had received" about activities at the facility.

The Attorney General's office confirmed this week it has received a request on behalf of the state conference of the NAACP to investigate the sheriff's office concerning allegations involving the facility.

The letter, signed by L.A. Warren, chairman of the Legal Redress Committee, of the state NAACP, asks the Attorney General's office to look into a number of allegations, including that Stringer allegedly made false allegations to cause the investigation into the regional facility.

During a meeting held last month at the Mississippi Rural Center in the Lampton community, Warren said formal complaints would be filed with the offices of the state Attorney General and the U.S. Department of Justice.

The NAACP's request comes on the heels of a lawsuit filed in the Southern District of U.S. District Court on Nov. 7 on behalf of Britton "Britt" Mosley Sr. the former assistant chief of security at the facility, against Marion County, the Marion County Sheriff's Department and Richard Stringer in his official capacity as sheriff of Marion County.

According to that suit, "Beginning in February 2001, immediately after his promotion, plaintiff Mosley was subjected to verbal harassment, physical threats and attempted conspiracy to plant illegal drugs in his possession."

The suit continues, "On or about Jan. 5, 2001, plaintiff Mosley filed charges of discrimination with the Equal Employment Opportunity Commission based on racial discrimination. On or about Feb. 26, 2001, plaintiff Mosley amended his charge of discrimination. On or about Aug. 11, 2001, plaintiff Mosley received a notice of right to sue..."

Mosley's suit requests any back pay owed, front pay (if necessary), compensatory damages of not less than $75,000, reasonable attorneys' fees and costs and other general relief deemed appropriate by the court.

L.A. Warren

The Columbian-Progress

Thursday, April 25, 2002 — 50 cents

AG will not pursue charges against fired prison workers

Letter says investigation uncovers minor wrongdoing by Daniels only

By Dana Gower
Staff Writer

A letter from the state Attorney General's office to Sheriff Richard "Rip" Stringer dated Jan. 16 states that "there will be no criminal charges or ethics violations pursued" against the former warden and assistant warden at the Marion/Walthall Correctional Facility.

Stringer fired former warden Jimmy Fancher and former assistant warden James Harvey last year, along with Britton "Britt" Mosley Sr., who had been working as assistant chief of security. A fourth employee, food service director Gennett Daniels, was originally cut back from a full-time employee to part-time before also being fired.

Stringer, who had earlier said he would not comment on the investigation before it was completed, could not be reached for comment Tuesday concerning the January letter.

The letter, signed by Special Assistant Attorney General Lee Martin, states, in part. "As you are aware, my office along with the Department of Corrections conducted an investigation concerning alleged wrongdoing at the Marion/Walthall County Correctional Facility. There were allegations that Warden Fancher and Assistant Warden Harvey were using the property of the facility and inmate labor for their personal benefit. As a result of our investigation, there will be no criminal charges or ethics violations pursued against either Fancher or Harvey. We are aware that you have terminated Fancher and Harvey from their positions with the correctional facility. In addition, you are aware that my office had no involvement in the decision to terminate them and your decision to terminate them was made independent of our investigation."

Contacted Tuesday, Martin said no criminal charges are being pursued against either Mosley, who is not mentioned in the Jan. 16 letter, or against Daniels.

Martin said that just because a criminal statute could apply to a

See Prison, Page 2

CHAPTER 9

Congressional Inquiry

Historically, most congressional representatives in Mississippi had not held up to their responsibilities of fairness and impartiality toward civil rights violations. Jimmy Fancher and Britton Mosley, Sr., are veterans of corrections and always held a healthy respect for the law and the judicial process. However, after the way their cases were ignored and summarily judgments dismissed by judges, and their lives and careers destroyed, they both find it difficult to believe in the civil and criminal justice systems in Mississippi.

They requested assistance from their US Congressional Representatives in Mississippi. The political representations at that time were Senate Trent Lot (South District), Senator Thad Cochran (North District), and Representative Gene Taylor (Fifth District).

They requested assistance from the US Department of Justice to initiate a civil rights investigation. Compelling evidence, audio tape, witness statements, and many documents could be provided. They felt the evidence would show that serious malfeasances had transpired in the handling of their cases by the justice system. The senator that represented Mosley, Senator Trent Lott, never responded to his request. Representative Gene Taylor made a request to the US Department of Justice Civil Rights Division. Senator Thad Cochran responded to Fancher's request. The US Department of Justice gave Senator Cochran a written response; however, the Department of Justice did not conduct an investigation (see attachments). This rejected investigation was a painful disappointment.

Britton Mosley, Sr. & John Fancher

GENE TAYLOR
5TH DISTRICT, Mississippi

COMMITTEE ON NATIONAL SECURITY

COMMITTEE ON TRANSPORTATION
AND INFRASTRUCTURE

Congress of the United States
House of Representatives
Washington, DC 20515-2405

2311 RAYBURN BUILDING
WASHINGTON, DC 20515-2405
(202) 225-5772

DISTRICT OFFICES:
2424 14TH ST.
GULFPORT, MS 39501
(228) 864-7670

701 MAIN ST.
SUITE 215
HATTIESBURG, MS 39401
(601) 582-3246

1215 B-GOVERNMENT ST.
OCEAN SPRINGS, MS 39564
(228) 872-7950

May 22, 2001

Brett Mosley
P.O. Box 390
State Line, MS 39362

Dear Brett:

    Thank you for contacting my office requesting assistance regarding the U.S. Department of Justice. Enclosed you will find a copy of the correspondence that I received from the Civil Rights Division on your behalf.

    Please know that it was my pleasure to be of service to you. If I can assist you further in this or any other matter, please feel free to contact my Hattiesburg District Office located at 701 Main Street – Suite 215, Hattiesburg, MS 39401.

With warm regards, I am

Sincerely yours,

GENE TAYLOR
Member of Congress

GT:jm

Enclosure

Fabricating Evidence II

U. S. Department of Justice

Civil Rights Division

Office of the Assistant Attorney General   Washington, D.C. 20530

MAY 2 2001

Captain Britton Mosley, Sr.
Marion/Walthall Correctional Facility
503 South Main Street
Columbia, MS 39429

Dear Captain Mosley:

    Congressman Gene Taylor has forwarded a copy of your letter dated February 21, 2001, requesting his assistance in securing an appointment to meet with the Attorney General to discuss issues regarding the Marion/Walthall Correctional Facility, to the Civil Rights Division for appropriate review and response.

    We regret that the Attorney General cannot meet with you at this time. However, we have carefully reviewed your correspondence. Your letter does not contain sufficient information relative to the issues you reference. If you are willing to provide specific details describing these issues, this matter will receive our careful consideration. Should it develop that a violation of federal law is involved, appropriate action will be taken.

    Please do not hesitate to contact the Department if we can be of assistance in other matters.

                                       Sincerely,

                                       William R. Yeomans
                                       Acting Assistant Attorney General
                                       Civil Rights Division

Britton Mosley, Sr. & John Fancher

James Harvey
415 Connor Avenue
Columbia, MS 39429
601-736-6746/601-731-2182

December 26, 2002

Senator Trent Lott
United States Senate
487 Russell Building
Washington, D.C. 20510

Dear Senator Lott:

My name is James Harvey, and I, along with Britton Mosley, Sr. are writing you this letter. We are both former employees of the Marion Walthall Correctional Facility in Columbia, MS. We have been keeping track of your current political situation and have concluded that while your comments were inappropriate and insensitive, that you should be afforded the opportunity to prove to the people of Mississippi and the nation that you are not, in fact, an insensitive or unjust person. That brings us to the purpose of this letter.

There is an ongoing situation here in Marion County Mississippi that reeks of racism and injustice. This situation involves Sheriff Richard Stringer and other members of the Marion County Sheriff's Department, the Mississippi Department of Corrections, and a member of the Mississippi Attorney General's Office.

This problem began in December of 2000, when a member of Sheriff Stringer's department was audio taped having a conversation with a county inmate wherein the sheriff's department officer conspired to falsely entrap me, James Harvey, former assistant warden of the Marion Walthall Correctional Facility on false drug charges. Upon receiving this information, I, an African-American male, filed complaints with the Equal Employment Opportunity Commission, the state NAACP, and Sheriff Stringer himself. Sheriff Stringer refused to take any disciplinary action against this employee because Sheriff Stringer himself was implicated in the setup. (See Transcript A)

In April of 2001, Sheriff Stringer requested and received a Mississippi Attorney General's and Mississippi Department of Corrections investigation of, Warden Jimmy Fancher, Captain Britton Mosely, and me, Assistant Warden James Harvey in retaliation for complaints having been filed by Mr. Mosely and me. In July of 2001, and during the course of this investigation, another audiotape was obtained of a conversation between an Attorney General's Office investigator, and three (3) members of the Marion County Sheriff's Department. In this conversation, the Attorney General investigator can be heard making graphic sexual comments about Warden Fancher, and the entire group racially profiles me, James Harvey, and other African-Americans in Corrections as all being "gang bangers." (See Transcript B)

On October 17, 2001, Sheriff Stringer fired Warden Fancher, Captain Mosely, Warden Fancher's secretary, Charlotte Broom, and me, James Harvey, without having the results of the investigation which he initiated. According to Sheriff Stringer, his reason for terminating each of us was because of the investigation.

Fabricating Evidence II

In March of 2002, Mr. L.A. Warren of the State NAACP requested and received the official conclusion to the Attorney General's report (see attached). The conclusion was that all persons terminated were exonerated of any wrongdoing either criminally or ethically. So the question, Mr. Lott is why were we fired from jobs that we had the experience and training to perform? The answer is – the racist views of Sheriff Stringer and others and his desire to retaliate against us for denouncing these views and actions.

We have heard you say, Senator Lott, any number of times on national television recently that you denounce racism and its ideals and that you will tirelessly fight against injustice in this country. Well, Senator Lott, we truly want to believe you when you say that because we believe that you are a fundamentally sound and decent person who has done a lot for the state of Mississippi. However, now some of your home state folk that you represent are in need of your help.

Senator, you can prove to the people of this great state as well as the people of the nation where you stand on the issue of racism and injustice. You can do it not with words but with action. We, James Harvey and Britton Mosely, Sr., are requesting that you do an inquiry into this matter we have just described to you. There is a lot more information on this subject which we will be glad to turn over to you at your request. The Bible states that *"Charity begins at home and then spreads abroad."* We are not asking for a handout, Senator just someone fair and impartial to thoroughly investigate this matter. We have not received this so far from the government agencies we have dealt with to date.

We thank you in advance for your time and attention to this matter, Senator Lott. We need some closure here in Marion County. We would like for you to set up a meeting between the aforementioned persons who were unjustly discriminated against and yourself at your earliest convenience. We feel that if you review the information that we can provide, you too will be convinced of the injustice. We anxiously await your response,

Sincerely,

James Harvey
James Harvey

Britton Mosely, Sr.
Britton Mosely, Sr.

Enclosures (2)

JMH/BM/lsh

Britton Mosley, Sr. & John Fancher

GENE TAYLOR
5TH DISTRICT, MISSISSIPPI

COMMITTEE ON NATIONAL SECURITY

COMMITTEE ON TRANSPORTATION
AND INFRASTRUCTURE

Congress of the United States
House of Representatives
Washington, DC 20515-2405

2311 RAYBURN BUILDING
WASHINGTON, DC 20515-24
(202) 225-5772

DISTRICT OFFICES:
2424 14TH ST.
GULFPORT, MS 39501
(228) 864-7670

701 MAIN ST.
SUITE 215
HATTIESBURG, MS 39401
(601) 582-3246

1215 B-GOVERNMENT ST.
OCEAN SPRINGS, MS 39564
(228) 872-7950

July 25, 2000

Britton Mosley
P.O. Box 390
State Line, MS 39362

Dear Britton:

    I have made a congressional inquiry to the U.S. Department of Justice and will continue to monitor this situation with great interest. Enclosed you will find a copy of the correspondence that was sent. As soon as I receive a reply, I will contact you.

    Meanwhile, if you have any questions or further information that would be helpful, please contact my District Representative, Mrs. Jerry Martin, in the Hattiesburg Office located at 701 Main Street – Suite 215, Hattiesburg, MS 39401 or call 1-800-273-4363 (582-3246).

Sincerely yours,

GENE TAYLOR
Member of Congress

GT:jm

Enclosure

Fabricating Evidence II

U.S. Department of Justice

Civil Rights Division

Office of the Assistant Attorney General   Washington, D.C. 20530

DEC 1 9 2011

The Honorable Thad Cochran
United States Senator
911 East Jackson Avenue, Suite 249
Oxford, Mississippi 38655

Dear Senator Cochran:

    This responds to your letter to the Assistant Attorney General for the Office of Legislative Affairs dated October 24, 2011 on behalf of your constituent, Mr. Jimmy Fancher, regarding alleged discriminatory and retaliatory acts committed against him by his former employer, the Marion-Walthall County/Regional Correctional Facility ("MWCF"). We apologize for the delay in responding.

    With your inquiry you enclosed a copy of correspondence and accompanying materials that Mr. Fancher sent to you concerning his allegations that he has been discriminated and retaliated against by his former employer, the MWCF, on the basis of his race. Specifically, Mr. Fancher alleges that MWCF officials lodged false accusations against him, which subsequently led to his discharge from employment as the MWCF warden. In response, Mr. Fancher requested an investigation by the Mississippi Office of Attorney General ("AG"). Although the investigation concluded that no ethics or criminal charges against Mr. Fancher were warranted, Mr. Fancher alleges that the investigators made racially derogatory and sexually inappropriate comments during the investigation. Mr. Fancher has filed a complaint with the Department of Justice and is seeking further assistance with this matter.

    Title VII of the Civil Rights Act of 1964, as amended, 42 U.S.C. § 2000e, *et seq.* ("Title VII"), prohibits discrimination in employment on the basis of race, color, sex, national origin and religion. Title VII also prohibits an employer from retaliating against an individual for opposing any employment practice that would violate Title VII, for filing a discrimination charge, or for assisting in the investigation of such a charge. Congress has designated the Equal Employment Opportunity Commission ("EEOC") as the federal agency responsible for investigating individual charges of discrimination under Title VII. If Mr. Fancher believes that the MWCF

183

The Honorable Thad Cochran
Page Two

discharged him from employment based on his race in violation of Title VII, he should, if he has not yet done so, contact the EEOC to find out whether he may file a charge. The EEOC may be called toll-free at 1-800-669-4000 or 1-800-669-6820 (TDD), which will connect Mr. Fancher to the EEOC office nearest him, or he may write to the following EEOC office:

> Equal Employment Opportunity Commission
> Dr. A. H. McCoy Federal Building
> 100 West Capitol Street, Suite 207
> Jackson, Mississippi 39269

It is important that a charge be filed with the EEOC as soon as possible, because a discrimination charge must be filed within a certain time period after the alleged discriminatory act occurred in order to be considered timely.

The Department of Justice has authority to pursue an individual charge of discrimination against a state or local government employer under Title VII only after the EEOC has determined that reasonable cause exists to believe a violation of Title VII has occurred, conciliation fails, and the EEOC refers the charge to us. When the EEOC refers charges to us, we give them careful consideration.

To the extent Mr. Fancher alleges, and local media coverage suggests, that his discharge was at least partially in retaliation for his opposition to state control over regional correctional facilities, that allegation does not implicate a federal statute with respect to which this Department has jurisdiction.

With respect to Mr. Fancher's allegation that the AG or its investigators have engaged in a racially discriminatory or otherwise inappropriate investigation, the Department of Justice does not have jurisdiction over the manner in which the AG's office investigates incidents involving regional correctional facilities. Ms. Pugh, with whom Mr. Fancher previously had discussions regarding this matter, is no longer employed by United States Attorney's Office in Mississippi. Moreover, Assistant United States Attorney Futloye, whom Mr. Fancher references in his letter, indicates that her office has no record of his complaint.

The Honorable Thad Cochran
Page Three

Mr. Fancher may wish to consult with a private attorney of his own choosing and at his own expense to determine what other remedies, if any, may be available to him. If Mr. Fancher is unable to afford a private attorney, he may desire to contact a local legal aid agency to find out whether it may be able to assist him.

We hope this information is helpful. Please do not hesitate to contact the Department if we may be of assistance regarding this, or any other, matter.

Sincerely,

Thomas E. Perez/js

Thomas E. Perez
Assistant Attorney General

CHAPTER 10

Mississippi Department of Corruption

The five-year federal investigation, "Mississippi Hustle," ended Chris Epps career as Mississippi's longest serving corrections commissioner. On November 5, 2014, after working four decades in the prison system, Chris Epps quit his job abruptly, without explanation. The following day, the news broke: Allegations of kickbacks for nearly $1 billion dollars' worth of private prison contracts, more than $1 million dollars in bribes, which led to a federal Investigation and indictment of former Mississippi Corrections Commissioner Chris Epps and former state lawman Cecil McCrory. Facing a 49-count indictment, the two men are accused of a scheme in which McCrory directed more than $1 million dollars to Epps, including cash and mortgage payments. In 2008, after McCrory sold GT Enterprises and Epps gave McCrory a favorable recommendation, McCrory sent $200,000 in payments to pay off mortgage that Epps had on his 3,800-square-foot home in Flowood, Mississippi with a $360,000 price tag. When the FBI arrested Epps, agents found $69,000 in cash in his safe. There was also about $1 million dollars in his investment retirement account.

An indicted county official, who committed suicide, had been targeted in the Mississippi Department of Corrections' corruption case. Harrison County Supervisor William Martin killed himself before dawn, hours before his scheduled arraignment of the federal indictment charging him with two counts of bribery and one count of witness tampering. Martin's indictment was an outgrowth of the corruption investigation that began with Chris Epps and Cecil McCrory. Two more men, Irb Benjamin and Sam Waggoner, were charged in the Mississippi Department of Corrections contract scandal involving Chris Epps. Benjamin and Waggoner were charged with paying bribes and kickback to Epps in exchange for receiving contracts involving the Mississippi Department of Corrections and its operations. The indictment alleges that Benjamin paid Epps for his help in getting Benjamin's company, Mississippi Correctional Management, consulting contracts. Those contracts involved Benjamin providing consulting services during the construction and the operations of regional corrections facilities. Benjamin's company provided consulting services to assist the regional corrections facilities in obtaining and maintaining accreditations by the American Correctional Association. Chris Epps was the former president of the American Correctional Association. In 2000, Benjamin provided the consulting services to the Marion/Walthall Correctional Facility during the ACA audit. Former Mississippi Corrections Commissioner Chris Epps pled guilty to two federal charges on February 25, 2015, and officials talked of more indictments in the continuing investigation.

"I'm sorry for what I've done," Epps told US District Judge Henry T. Wingate, "I repented before God. I apologize to my family and the state of Mississippi." Epps, who was originally indicted on 40 counts of bribery, money laundering, conspiracy and tax charges, also pled guilty to filing a false tax return for tax year 2008. Epps pled guilty to telling the IRS he earned only $205,540 when he actually earned at least $405,540. Epps faces a maximum prison sentence by statute of 23 years and a $750,000 fine.

On June 8, 2015, Chris Epps' sentencing was delayed indefinitely, according to federal court officials. An official in US District Judge Wingate's office confirmed the sentencing was delayed. Epps must cooperate with federal prosecutors as part of his plea, and prosecutors typically delay sentencing until cooperation is complete. Indictment of Chris Epps exposed systematic and invasive corruption inside the Mississippi Department of Corrections and the Marion County Sheriff's Department. Jimmy Fancher and Britton Mosley, Sr., exposed this corruption, and their careers in law enforcement were destroyed. They became targets of the Mississippi Department of Corrections, the Office of the Attorney General and the Marion County Sheriff's Department. This collusion by these law enforcement agencies attempted a wrongful conviction of Fancher and Mosley, based on fabricated evidence.

The abuse of power and cover-up by former Attorney General Mike Moore created a "culture of corruption" inside the Mississippi Department of Corrections and the Marion County Sheriff's Department. Mike Moore was the Attorney General of the state of Mississippi from 1988 to 2004. During that time, Moore was the attorney for the Mississippi Department of Corrections, which was a conflict of interest. The Office of the Attorney General should have withdrawn from the investigation at the Marion/Walthall Corrections Facility. It is alleged under Chris Epps' leadership that Mike Moore's law firm received millions in payments on non-bidding contracts with the Mississippi

Department of Corrections. The evidence in this book shows and explains how the Office of the Attorney General denied Fancher and Mosley their Fourteenth Amendment Right: deny to any person within its jurisdiction the equal protection of the laws.

Fabricating Evidence II

MDOC official: Corruption "deep and wide"

JOURNEY TO JUSTICE (//WWW.CLARIONLEDGER.COM/BLOG/JOURNEYTOJUSTICE/)   Jerry Mitchell, The Clarion-Ledger   3:02 p.m. CST November 6, 2014

Chris Epps *(Photo: The Clarion-Ledger)*

A Mississippi Department of Corrections official recently told me that corruption inside is "both deep and wide."

On Thursday, Chris Epps, who abruptly resigned as the $132,000-a-year Corrections Commissioner a day before, pleaded not guilty to an indictment that he received more than $700,000 in bribes that helped him pay off his $380,000 home and beach condo.

Federal officials are now moving to seize them as well as his two Mercedes-Benz sedans.

The Clarion-Ledger's series "A Hard Look at Hard Time" revealed a prison system in Mississippi, where gangs rule, where corruption festers and where prison serves as "a college for criminality."

Such corruption has included gangs extorting the families of inmates. Gang members have also paid correctional officers to not only smuggle in drugs and other contraband, but also to do favors for gangs, including allegedly "popping" locks to enable assaults and killings.

THE CLARION LEDGER
The Clarion-Ledger Hard Look At Hard Time Section

(http://www.clarionledger.com/news/hard-look/?from=global&sessionKey=&autologin=)

The annual starting pay for a correctional officer in Mississippi is $22,006, which more than qualifies their family of three for food stamps.

Janna Bridges, who worked as a corrections officer for eight years at the Central Mississippi Correctional Facility, told The Clarion-Ledger that an inmate approached her, saying, "We can improve your salary a whole lot if you will make a few trips into Jackson for me."

She refused but saw some officers succumb to temptation, she said. "You can see corruption. It's everywhere."

Inmates pop pills and smoke marijuana, meth, crack and spice, she said. "I don't know of any drug that didn't make the door and come on in. It was a free-flowing retail store out there."

Inmates even gave one officer the nickname "Mr. Cocaine," she said.

191

She knew about sex between officers and inmates, knew about officers making thousands from contraband they brought in, she said. "You know so much, but you can't report it."

If officers did, drugs or something else might be planted inside their cars, she said. "You can't talk about a lot of stuff."

After Clifton Majors was killed in 2013 inside the Central Mississippi Correctional Facility, his mother, Brenda Moreno, said she and her husband voiced concerns to Epps about corruption inside the prison.

Epps acknowledged the problem, she said. "I was thinking if you know, why aren't you doing something about it?"

She said when she discussed the problem of corruption among the officers, Epps replied, "Well, you've got to understand these people are uneducated and underpaid."

She said he went on to suggest the officers took such money to supplement their income.

When I asked Epps if low pay made officers more susceptible to bribes, he responded in a now ironic remark: "I believe it's the character of the individual that makes a person susceptible to many things."

He denied that gangs were powerful inside Mississippi prisons.

In fact, he told me his department doesn't recognize gangs. "These inmates are identified as Security Threat Groups," he said. "The inmates are classified appropriately, following the national trend of correctional practitioners."

As one official put it to me, "The gangs are running the prisons. The guards just happen to have the keys."

Read or Share this story: http://on.thec-l.com/1u4dGdh

Fabricating Evidence II

Chris Epps, Cecil McCrory plead guilty to corruption

Former Mississippi Corrections Commissioner Chris Epps apologizes after pleading guilty to two federal charges Wednesday, Feb. 25, 2015 in Jackson, Miss. C. Todd Sherman/The Clarion-Ledger

Jerry Mitchell and Jimmie E. Gates, The Clarion-Ledger   9:06 a.m. CST February 26, 2015

(Photo: Joe Ellis/The Clarion-Ledger)

Former Mississippi Corrections Commissioner Chris Epps pleaded guilty to two federal charges Wednesday — and officials talked of more indictments in the continuing investigation.

"I'm sorry for what I've done," Epps told U.S. District Judge Henry T. Wingate. "I've repented before God. I apologize to my family and the state of Mississippi."

He first met Cecil McCrory in 1997 when he was serving in the Mississippi Legislature. "He gave me gratuities," said Epps, who was working for the state Department of Corrections but was not yet commissioner.

In 2008, after McCrory sold GT Enterprises and Epps gave McCrory a favorable recommendation, McCrory sent $200,000 in payments to pay off the mortgage that Epps had on his 3,800-square-foot home in Flowood with a $360,000 price tag, Epps said.

McCrory, who also pleaded guilty Wednesday, said Epps was the one who approached him about paying off the Flowood home. "He talked me into making that first payment," he told the judge. "It's something I never thought I would do, but I can't take it back."

Assistant U.S. Attorney Mike Hurst of Jackson described how Epps used that home equity to take out a loan for a condominium in Biloxi. After McCrory paid off that condo, Epps used that equity to get a bigger condominium in Pass Christian.

Epps, who was originally indicted on 40 counts of bribery, money laundering, conspiracy and tax charges, also pleaded guilty to filing a false tax return for tax year 2008. Epps pled guilty to telling the IRS he earned only $205,540 when he actually received at least $405,540.

McCrory pleaded guilty Wednesday to being a part of the same money laundering conspiracy. If Epps had not pleaded, McCrory would have been a witness against him.

McCrory told the judge that he had received $2 million directly from the state Department of Corrections and another $3 million as a consultant for other companies.

Britton Mosley, Sr. & John Fancher

Two businessmen charged with bribing Chris Epps

The Clarion-Ledger 11:45 a.m. CDT August 21, 2015

(Photo: The Clarion-Ledger)

Release put out by the U.S. Attorney's office in Jackson:

TWO MISSISSIPPI BUSINESSMEN CHARGED WITH BRIBERY OF FORMER CORRECTIONS COMMISSIONER

JACKSON – Irb Benjamin, 69, of Madison, and Sam Waggoner, 61, of Carthage, were charged today (Aug. 21) with paying bribes and kickbacks to former Mississippi Department of Corrections Commissioner (MDOC) Christopher B. Epps in exchange for receiving contracts involving the MDOC and its operations, announced Acting United States Attorney Harold Brittain, FBI Special Agent in Charge (SAC) Donald Alway, IRS-Criminal Investigation Special Agent in Charge Jerome McDuffie, U.S. Postal Inspector Robert Wemyss, and Mississippi State Auditor Stacey Pickering.

Benjamin was charged in a three count indictment returned by a federal grand jury with conspiracy to commit honest services wire fraud and with two counts of bribery. According to the indictment returned against Benjamin, from some time in 2010 until September, 2014, Benjamin gave Epps bribes and kickbacks in exchange for Epps awarding or directing the awarding of MDOC contracts or work to Benjamin's company, Mississippi Correctional Management (MCM), to provide alcohol and drug treatment services to inmates at MDOC work centers in Alcorn and Simpson Counties. MCM was paid about $774,000.00 as a result of those contracts.

The indictment alleges that Benjamin paid Epps for Epps' help in getting MCM consulting contracts with Alcorn, Washington and Chickasaw Counties. Those contracts involved Benjamin providing consulting services during the construction and the subsequent operation of three regional corrections facilities. Benjamin purportedly provided consulting services to assist the regional corrections facilities in obtaining and maintaining accreditation by the American Correctional Association. The contract with Alcorn County paid MCM about $399,260.00; the contract with Washington County paid MCM about $245,080.00; and, the contract with Chickasaw County paid MCM about $217,900.00.

The indictment also alleges that Benjamin paid Epps monthly kickbacks from the consultant fees Benjamin received from Carter Gobal Lee Facility Management (CGL), after CGL obtained a contract in 2014 to provide maintenance services to MDOC facilities. Epps used his influence over CGL to get Benjamin the job as a consultant for CGL. The value of the CGL contract was $4,800,000.

Waggoner was charged by Criminal Information with one count of bribery related to his payments of bribes and kickbacks to Epps from sometime in 2012 until at least August 26, 2014. According to the Criminal Information, Waggoner was a consultant for Global Tel-Link (GTL), which provided telephone services at MDOC facilities. The Criminal Information cites two

specific instances in 2014 where Waggoner paid Epps kickbacks from money Waggoner received from GTL as a consultant.

Harold Brittain, Acting U.S. Attorney in this case, stated: "The abuse of power and position by public officials has plagued our state for many years. Our tolerance for public corruption is zero. We will hold accountable under the law everyone who bears the responsibility of public service and sells the trust that has been bestowed upon them. We will not tolerate such fraud and abuses by public officials that have cost our citizens so dearly."

In commenting on this case, FBI SAC Donald Alway applauded the investigators and prosecutors, whose hard work and determined efforts revealed these additional participants in this conspiracy of public corruption, and led to the charges announced today. He added, "Our society will not tolerate bribery, kickbacks, or other 'under-the-table' deals. This is not just another cost of doing business with government. The FBI, working alongside its law enforcement partners, will use every appropriate tool and available resource to find, stop, and punish those who conspire to betray the public trust in order to enrich themselves."

THE CLARION LEDGER

Former MDOC Commissioner Chris Epps' sentencing delayed

(http://www.clarionledger.com/story/news/2015/06/08/epps-mdoc-sentencing-delayed/28695761/)

Fabricating Evidence II

"Postal Inspectors bring to a task force unique skills for hunting down suspected fraud through the U.S. Mail," said U.S. Postal Inspector in Charge Adrian Gonzalez. "Postal Inspectors steadfastly work with our partners and defend the nation's mail system in hopes that criminals abusing the American public's trust are brought to justice."

Special Agent Jerome R. McDuffie, IRS – Criminal Investigation, stated: "This is a very important investigation to the state of Mississippi and all individuals who rely on the trust they instill in their public officials, whether elected or appointed. The extent to which Christopher Epps has damaged that trust will require as much effort to rebuild as it did to uncover. The Special Agents of IRS – Criminal Investigation remain committed to working with our law enforcement partners in uncovering public corruption at even the highest levels of government, as well holding accountable those individuals involved."

"We will continue to fight public corruption in Mississippi and work with our partners," said State Auditor Pickering. "Our agents and this team are working daily to identify and bring charges against all individuals associated with the Mississippi Department of Corrections case. I'd like to thank the U.S. Attorney's Office, FBI, IRS, and the U.S. Postal Service for a joint effort in this ongoing case."

Both defendants are scheduled to make their initial appearances before U.S. Magistrate Judge F. Keith Ball on Friday, August 21, 2015, at 1:30 p.m. Waggoner faces a maximum penalty of 10 years in prison and a $250,000.00 fine, as well as forfeiture of the proceeds he obtained as a result of the illegal conduct. Benjamin faces a maximum penalty of 20 years in prison and a $250,000.00 fine for the conspiracy count, and a maximum of 10 years in prison and a $250,000.00 fine for each of the bribery counts. Benjamin also faces the forfeiture of his ill-gotten gains.

This case was investigated by the Federal Bureau of Investigation, U.S. Postal Inspection Service, Mississippi State Auditor's Office and IRS Criminal Investigation. It is being prosecuted by Deputy Criminal Chief Darren LaMarca, Assistant United States Attorney Scott Gilbert, and financial analyst Kim Mitchell.

Read or Share this story: http://on.thec-l.com/1NK4VfF

Britton Mosley, Sr. & John Fancher

U.S. District Judge Carlton Reeves recently ruled that the Mississippi Department of Corrections still has a ways to go in cleaning up Walnut Grove prison and left a consent decree in place so that a court could monitor MDOC's progress. Photo by Imani Khayyam.

Legal advocates for prisoners in Mississippi say the state has failed to follow through on promises to create better conditions at Walnut Grove Correctional Facility and that attempts to address safety concerns at Walnut Grove, which started out as a youth prison, have spurred violence at other prisons.

Jody Owens, managing attorney for the Southern Poverty Law Center's Mississippi office, said Wilkinson County Correctional Facility in Woodville is now the most violent prison in the state.

The problems at Wilkinson County are a direct result of the Mississippi Department of Corrections' response to a 2012 federal court settlement at Walnut Grove that required MDOC to improve conditions and reduce violence at the facility.

In response, MDOC slashed the population of Walnut Grove by one-third. Wilkinson

Fabricating Evidence II

County is one of the prisons where close-custody prisoners were sent in what Owens characterizes as a smoke-and-mirrors move to make MDOC appear as if the agency was complying with the Walnut Grove order.

"When we look at this whack-a-mole, we have to ask ourselves what is the root the problems," Owens said.

In his opinion, the root is in the arrangement between MDOC and the private companies it hires to run the facilities. One of those companies, Centerville, Utah-based Management & Training Corporation, holds four such contracts, including for Walnut Grove and Wilkinson County. MTC also runs prisons in Marshall and Lauderdale counties; Correctional Corporation of America holds one contract, for Tallahatchie County Correctional Facility.

Management & Training Corp., which manages the prison, said in a statement that the company and MDOC has made good-faith efforts to address issues raised in the consent decree, including removing children and seriously mentally ill prisoners. MTC also said the facility is safe, secure, clean and accredited by the American Correctional Association. In addition, the prison has eliminated long-term segregation and high-security-risk prisoners.

In doing so, MDOC unsuccessfully asked a federal judge this spring to lift the court order. In an ordered handed down last week, U.S. District Judge Carlton Reeves wrote that prisoners' rights continued to be exposed to "current and ongoing violations."

Reeves heard arguments in April in a case over a federal consent decree at Walnut Grove, which a private prison company manages on behalf of the Mississippi Department of Corrections.

The judge's order, issued June 10, leaves the consent decree in place.

In its defense, MDOC argued that Walnut Grove has since cleaned up its act since the 2010 lawsuit was filed. "It's not the same facility I found when I arrived," Lepher

Jenkins, who took over as warden at Walnut Grove after a July 2014 uprising that sent a number of prisoners to the hospital, testified during the hearing.

Attorneys for prisoners, from the ACLU National Prison Project and the Southern Poverty Law Center, said the conditions that first brought the lawsuit persist. Owens points to a number of "spice" (synthetic marijuana) overdoses at Walnut Grove in the weeks before hearing.

During the hearing, two prisoners testified about what they called unsafe conditions at Walnut Grove and the mistreatment of inmates by MDOC officials. This treatment continued during their time in custody at the Central Mississippi Correctional Facility in early April, when plaintiffs argued their case. The defendant, MDOC, put on its case three weeks later.

Judge Reeves, in his ruling, agreed with the plaintiffs.

"We know that most prisoners do not die in prison; they serve their sentences and are subsequently released. How they are treated while in prison affects how they will reintegrate into society upon their release. As such, public confidence in our criminal justice and public safety systems is vital," he wrote.

MDOC has not indicated whether the agency will appeal Reeves' decision. With another SPLC lawsuit pending against East Mississippi Correctional Facility in Meridian, Owens said it would be in the best interests of the agency to negotiate rather than fighting the lawsuits in court.

"We want to find a way to avoid litigation we would hope the state would be responsible," Owens said.

CONCLUSION

The primary objective of the Mississippi Department of Corrections is correction. The concept of correction is the treatment and rehabilitation of offenders through a program involving penal custody. However, this book shows and explains how staff of the Mississippi Department of Corrections, the Office of the Attorney General, and the Marion County Sheriff's Department redefines this concept. The integrity meltdown of these agencies, and the abuse of power working collectively in order to get a successful outcome of an investigation, based on fabricated evidence, Former Warden Jimmy Fancher and former Captain Britton Mosley, Sr., were victims of this culture of corruption. *Merriam-Webster Collegiate Dictionary* defines the word *integrity* as being *incorruptibility*.

From John Fancher:
Three months before my eighteenth birthday, I volunteered to serve in the United States Marine Corps. After basic training

at Camp Lejeune, I volunteered to serve in Vietnam. While serving in Vietnam, I went from an eighteen-year-old kid to an aged adult in a very short time. After receiving several medals and an honorable discharge from the Marine Corps, I continued to serve and protect the people in America. So, it was no surprise when I started a law enforcement career with the Mississippi Department of Corrections.

The failed attempt to falsely incarcerate me by former Corrections Commissioner Chris Epps and fellow law enforcement personnel was emotionally devastating. Epps and I were co-workers (correctional officers) at the Mississippi State Penitentiary in Parchman, Mississippi. I never thought that refusing a bribe would lead to this betrayal of trust by Chris Epps.

During my second combat tour in Vietnam, I was wounded and I received the Purple Heart. After recovering from my injuries, my mental toughness was off the chain. However, my Vietnam experience did not prepare me for what it felt like to be betrayed by staff members inside the Marion County Sheriff's Department, the Mississippi Department of Corrections, and the Office of the Attorney General. In Vietnam, I knew who my enemies were, but not in Mississippi, I did not.

Fabricating Evidence II

From Britton Mosley, Sr.:

Fabricating Evidence: Drug Set-up/Cover-Up of a Correctional Whistleblower and *Fabricating Evidence II: Office of the Attorney General/Mississippi Department of Corrections Integrity Meltdown* were written to expose the corruption inside the Mississippi Department of Corrections, Marion County Sherriff's Department, and the Office of the Attorney General. John "Jimmy" Fancher and I were deliberately targeted to be falsely incarcerated, based on fabricated evidence.

This failed collusion between these law enforcement agencies ended our careers and created emotional and financial hardship. Being victimized by law enforcement personnel operating under the color law still angers and saddens us. It is worth mentioning that in Chapter 2 of *Fabricating Evidence: Drug Set-up/Cover-Up of a Correctional Whistleblower,* I wrote about my interview with former the Mississippi Department of Corrections Integrity Investigator Larry Smith, who offered me a bribe from former Corrections Commissioner Steve Puckett, of which I angrily declined. Also, in Chapter 3 of *Fabricating Evidence II: Office of the Attorney General/Mississippi Department of Corrections Integrity Meltdown,* former Corrections Commissioner Chris Epps offered John Fancher a bribe, of which he angrily declined.

Epps and Puckett were co-workers at the Mississippi State Penitentiary in Parchman, Mississippi, and are alleged to be close friends.

After refusing Puckett's and Epps' bribery attempts, Fancher and I were the targets of a wrongful prosecution attempt by the Office of the Attorney General. During the time these failed attempts were made, Mike Moore was the Attorney General. Also, it is alleged that Puckett, Epps, and Moore are friends.

Former Mississippi Department of Corrections Commissioner Chris Epps pled guilty to corruption charges, and faces a maximum prison sentence by statute of twenty-three years and a $750,000 fine. #KARMA

Fabricating Evidence: Drug Set-up/Cover-Up of a Correctional Whistleblower and *Fabricating Evidence II: Office of the Attorney General/Mississippi Department of Corrections Integrity Meltdown* shows and explains the integrity melt down inside the Mississippi Department of Corrections and the Office of the Attorney General. These two state agencies' investigators are called "integrity investigators," incorruptibility and honesty. However, they worked collectively to end your careers and turn your life upside down. We were blackballed, making securing gainful employment extremely difficult. Exposing corruption inside the Mississippi

Department of Corrections and the Attorney General's Office was economic suicide for Fancher and me, almost costing us our freedom. Our Fourteenth Amendment right for "equal protection under the law" was denied by people who are supposed to "serve and protect" us from criminal acts.

Jimmy Fancher's and my intentions are that our experiences will convince the American people of the need for criminal justice reform in Mississippi. It is time these agencies are held accountable for this "culture of corruption."

The federal criminal justice grant program was subsidizing mass incarceration in Mississippi. The grant money led to more arrests, more prosecution, and more imprisonment of African Americans on nonviolent drug charges in Mississippi. The money primarily was distributed to local law enforcement. This money created scandals and mass arrests by drug task forces based on evidence fabrication. African American families were targeted for this unjust incarceration.

The Office of the Attorney General allowed staff members inside the Mississippi Department of Corrections to operate "above the law" and created a "culture of corruption."

The criminal justice system in Mississippi has redefined and given slavery a new name: mass incarceration.

The mass incarceration of African Americans was achieved by the so-called "war on drugs." In Mississippi, nonviolent drug offenders can meet the requirements to provide free labor statewide. This new method of slave-making technique has damaged the family unit inside the African American community. It's ironic how history is representing itself one-hundred-fifty years (December 6, 1865 – December 6, 2015) after the Thirteenth Amendment to the United States Constitution that abolished slavery was ratified.

Mike Moore was Mississippi's Attorney General from 1988 to 2004. During that era, Moore became popular and powerful; his alliance with former President Bill Clinton and former Senator Trent Lott employed him politically. The former Chief Prosecutor of the state of Mississippi abused his power when he allowed staff members inside the Mississippi Department of Corrections and Marion County Sheriff's Department to operate under the color of law to commit criminal misconduct.

The Mississippi Department of Finance and Administrative data report/no-bid state contracts inside the Mississippi Department of Corrections (2010-2014) shows large sums of money was paid to the Mike Moore Law Firm. Former

Corrections Commissioner, and convicted felon, Chris Epps was the commissioner during that period. #BROKENTRUST

"Mass incarceration skyrocketed on September 13, 1994 when President Bill Clinton signed the Crime Bill of 1994 after Congress passed the bill in November of 1993. This bill was sought to begin the "war on drugs" in America, but it only resulted to an increasing number of inmates in prison as law enforcement received federal funding and the targeting of African American males became the main citizen to become victimized by this bill. The Crime Bill has been compared to modern-day slavery due to the huge influx of African American men receiving outrageous sentencing versus other races for the same crime. This action caused an outpouring number of innocent and guilty blacks to be imprisoned with undeserving prison time."

To learn more, visit our YouTube channel:
https://www.youtube.com/user/MDOCDrugSetUpCoverUp

ABOUT THE AUTHORS

Britton Mosley, Sr., is retired and resides in Northern Virginia.

John "Jimmy Fancher" is retired and resides in Northern Mississippi.

www.ingramcontent.com/pod-product-compliance
Lightning Source LLC
Chambersburg PA
CBHW020649300426
44112CB00007B/310